Essentials of Administering Team Foundation Server 2015

Using TFS 2015 to Accelerate Your Software Development

Gary Gauvin

Apress®

Essentials of Administering Team Foundation Server 2015: Using TFS 2015 to Accelerate Your Software Development

ISBN-13 (pbk): 978-1-4842-0572-3

ISBN-13 (electronic): 978-1-4842-0571-6

Managing Director: Welmoed Spahr
Development Editor: Douglas Pundick
Lead Editor: James DeWolf
Technical Reviewer: Fabio Cladio Ferracchiati
Editorial Board: Steve Anglin, Pramila Balen, Louise Corrigan, Jim DeWolf, Jonathan Gennick, Robert Hutchinson, Celestin Suresh John, Michelle Lowman, James Markham, Susan McDermott, Matthew Moodie, Jeffrey Pepper, Douglas Pundick, Ben Renow-Clarke, Gwenan Spearing
Coordinating Editor: Melissa Maldonado
Copy Editor: Kim Burton
Compositor: SPi Global
Indexer: SPi Global
Artist: SPi Global

Distributed to the book trade worldwide by Springer Science+Business Media New York, 233 Spring Street, 6th Floor, New York, NY 10013. Phone 1-800-SPRINGER, fax (201) 348-4505, e-mail orders-ny@springer-sbm.com, or visit www.springer.com. Apress Media, LLC is a California LLC and the sole member (owner) is Springer Science + Business Media Finance Inc (SSBM Finance Inc). SSBM Finance Inc is a Delaware corporation.

For information on translations, please e-mail rights@apress.com, or visit www.apress.com.

Apress and friends of ED books may be purchased in bulk for academic, corporate, or promotional use. eBook versions and licenses are also available for most titles. For more information, reference our Special Bulk Sales–eBook Licensing web page at www.apress.com/bulk-sales.

Any source code or other supplementary material referenced by the author in this text is available to readers at www.apress.com. For detailed information about how to locate your book's source code, go to www.apress.com/source-code/.

Contents at a Glance

About the Author xi

About the Technical Reviewer xiii

Acknowledgments xv

Introduction xvii

■Chapter 1: Planning for Team Foundation Server 1

■Chapter 2: Installing Team Foundation Server 13

■Chapter 3: Installation Validation and Security 45

■Chapter 4: Managing Collections... 67

■Chapter 5: Managing Team Projects.. 97

■Chapter 6: Managing Source Code and Work 119

■Chapter 7: Maintaining Team Foundation Server 143

■Chapter 8: Build Management 155

■Chapter 9: Testing with Team Foundation Server 165

■Chapter 10: Reporting and Other Features Worth Exploring 177

Index... 185

Contents

About the Author xi

About the Technical Reviewer xiii

Acknowledgments xv

Introduction xvii

■Chapter 1: Planning for Team Foundation Server 1

Before You Begin 1

Team Foundation Server 2013 Editions 1

TFS Architecture Overview 2

Installation Considerations 3

Basic Requirements 3

Installation Checklist 3

Accounts and Permissions 4

Supported Operating System Requirements 6

Performance and Planning 7

Hardware 8

Scaling Tips: One to Many 8

SharePoint Requirements 8

SQL Server Requirements 8

Active Directory 10

Ports 11

Language Requirements 12

Summary 12

■Chapter 2: Installing Team Foundation Server 13

Install Categories.. 13

New Install... 13

Upgrades 15

TFS Upgrade Scenarios 16

Back Up! 16

Installation Experience 20

SQL Reporting Services Configuration Manager 37

Summary.. 43

■Chapter 3: Installation Validation and Security 45

Installation Validation 45

Validate Team Foundation Server URLs.. 45

Validate TFS Services 48

Installation Logs 49

XAML Build Service 50

Team Foundation Server Security 61

Security Model... 62

Summary.. 65

■Chapter 4: Managing Collections... 67

Collections and Projects Overview 67

What Are They?.. 68

Collection Naming Convention... 69

Setting Up and Managing Team Project Collections....................................... 69

Team Project Collections 69

Summary.. 96

■Chapter 5: Managing Team Projects... 97

Team Projects Overview.. 97

Team Project Boundaries 98

Team Project Naming Conventions... 98

Setting up Team Projects... 98

Reporting Services Permissions to View or Create Reports 99

SQL Server Database Roles for Report Authors and to Create Team Projects 101

Check to Make Sure That You Are in the Project Collection Administrators Group 105

SharePoint Permissions.. 108

Team Project Security... 110

Pick a Process 110

Source Control Choices 110

Setting up a Team Project... 111

Summary 118

■Chapter 6: Managing Source Code and Work 119

Working with Source Code: Workspaces 119

Server or Local? 119

Setting up the Workspace... 120

Adding a Solution/Project to a Team Project 124

Checking In and Out 128

Branching and Merging 128

Managing Work 133

Setting up a Team... 133

Summary 142

■Chapter 7: Maintaining Team Foundation Server 143

Get Up to Date 143

Disk Space 144

Security! Microsoft Baseline Security Analyzer (MBSA) 144

Antivirus 144

IIS Process Exclusion... 144

SQL and SharePoint... 144

SQL Maintenance 145

    Backup 145

    Run DBCC CHECKDB 145

Backup 145

    Scheduled Backups Wizard 146

Summary 154

■**Chapter 8: Build Management** **155**

Overview 155

Setting up a Build Agent 155

Scaling and Administering Team Foundation Build 158

    Starting/Restarting Build Agents 158

    Settings: Build Retention 159

    Security: Letting Others Help Manage the Builds 159

Using Team Foundation Build 160

    Build Definitions: Creating and Queueing 161

Summary 164

■**Chapter 9: Testing with Team Foundation Server** **165**

Do I Need Visual Studio for My Dedicated QA Team/Testers? 165

Manual Test Planning, Creating, and Running 166

Continuous Integration Testing 174

Summary 175

■**Chapter 10: Reporting and Other Features Worth Exploring** **177**

SQL Reporting Services Reports 177

SharePoint Dashboards 179

Excel Reports 180

Other TFS Features You Should Explore 181

Lab Management 181

Release Management 181

ALM Virtual Machines 183

Summary 184

Index **185**

About the Author

Gary Gauvin is currently the Director of Application Lifecycle Management at CD-adapco, the leading provider of CFD (computational fluid dynamics) software. Gauvin has held senior positions in many of nation's top companies, as well as the consulting firm he founded.

Gauvin has worked in software development for over 20 years, spanning many industries and disciplines. He has been a Microsoft MVP in the ALM specialty, working closely with Microsoft on various releases of Team Foundation Server. He has consulted and worked for the nation's top technology companies. Gary lives and works in northern New Hampshire. You can follow his blog at www.theCTO.org. Feel free to connect with him on LinkedIn at www.linkedin.com/in/garypgauvin.

About the Technical Reviewer

Fabio Claudio Ferracchiati is a senior consultant and a senior analyst/developer using Microsoft technologies. He works for Blu Arancio (`www.bluarancio.com`). He is a Microsoft Certified Solution Developer for .NET, a Microsoft Certified Application Developer for .NET, a Microsoft Certified Professional, and a prolific author and technical reviewer. Over the past ten years, he's written articles for Italian and international magazines and coauthored more than ten books on a variety of computer topics.

Acknowledgments

I would like to thank my family for again putting up with the long hours and short deadlines a book like this requires. I'd also like to thank my co-workers for putting up with my ranting and raving about this book and occasionally pitching in with some editing. Finally, I'd like to thank the Apress team (especially Jim, Melissa, Douglas, and Fabio) for their help with the editing, formatting, and keeping things on track. Without them, this book would have never been completed.

Introduction

Who This Book Is For

The book is written for anyone who wants to get started quickly with Team Foundation Server. While not intended to be an exhaustive deep dive, it will provide the system administrator or development manager with enough detail to begin using TFS in their environment or provide a good jumping-off point for further study, if needed.

What You Will Learn

This book covers the critical as well as the less obvious aspects of managing Microsoft Team Foundation Server 2015 in a variety of development and test environments. Coverage includes basic installation, initial configuration, maintenance, valuable tips, sizing, and performance considerations.

Essentials of Administering Team Foundation Server 2015 explains how TFS can help you incorporate project management, source control, build automation, and testing in your development environment. You'll also learn how to set up TFS to match how you develop software.

The book covers TFS through the whole development process, along with practical advice on how to use its features effectively to get up to speed quickly.

In addition, the author dives into using TFS in your team, covering subjects like setting up accounts for different roles, users, and groups, plus what you need to know about TFS security and running a secure team.

No discussion of a centralized system like TFS would be complete without learning how to back up and restore it. The author covers what you need to know to maintain TFS, including the backup and restore details required to properly plan for disaster recovery.

The book details what you need to know about TFS functionality in creating and setting up collections and projects, how to manage the build process with team build (including setting it up and deploying build server and agents), using templates to speed up the creation of builds, building multiplatform solutions, and testing. It finishes up with a discussion on reporting and hints on additional areas to explore.

CHAPTER 1

■ ■ ■

Planning for Team Foundation Server

This chapter explores what you need to consider for establishing a solid Team Foundation Server (TFS) environment, including the following:

- General installation requirements

- Accounts and permissions needed

- Correctly sizing the environment

- Supported operating system requirements

- Specific SharePoint requirements

- SQL Server requirements

- Ports required

- Language considerations

Before You Begin

By using Team Foundation Server 2013, teams can enable themselves to get more productive faster and scale beyond a small team into a larger one, without outgrowing the toolset they are on. I am assuming that you have a functioning network and Windows Server installations to cover the infrastructure portions required for the installation. Also, it's probably worth pointing out that this book is based on Team Foundation Server 2013 Update 3, which was released on August 4, 2014. So if you are using a different edition, please make sure that you double-check the requirements for that release before you begin.

Team Foundation Server 2013 Editions

Team Foundation Server 2013 (TFS 2013) is available from a multitude of sources and at many price points, and as soon as I write this, Microsoft will probably add another one. Some popular ways to acquire it are free (Team Foundation Server 2013 Express is free for up to five users), a Microsoft Developer Network (MSDN) subscription, and various Microsoft Volume Licensing programs. If you don't want to host the server-side components within your organization, another alternative is to use Visual Studio Online. Not sure which is right for you? Your best bet is to first download and read the *Visual Studio 2015 and MSDN Licensing White Paper* available at www.microsoft.com/en-us/download/details.aspx?id=13350.

1

TFS Architecture Overview

Since TFS has a lot of moving parts, I thought I'd give you a picture of how it all fits together. Now before I get a lot of hate mail on this, it is a simplified chart and I'm likely going to leave off someone's favorite feature. All the big pieces are here though. The purpose is to the give the reader a better idea of how what's being discussed fits in the big TFS picture.

There are also a number of deployment options that will have an effect on the final look of your architecture, such as scaled-out servers and high availability (HA) database options (see Figure 1-1). This should serve as a good general reference, though, as you move through the book.

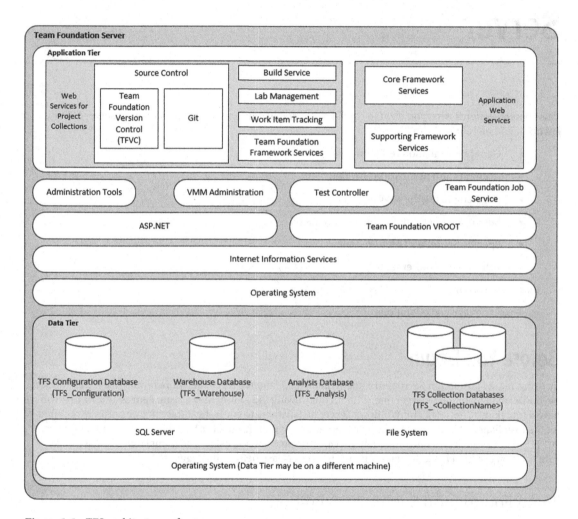

Figure 1-1. *TFS architecture reference*

Installation Considerations

There are a few pieces of information that you need to collect, and a few configuration tasks that you'll need to make sure have been completed properly. Here I'll cover the system requirements and provide a handy checklist that you can use so you aren't hunting around for critical information when you are anxious to begin.

Basic Requirements

One "new" requirement for this release is a 64-bit server operating system (OS). I know this is really not "new" news for everyone, but if you haven't had to install or upgrade an operating system in a while, this may come as a surprise. Also, you may require different hardware to support a 64-bit operating system (check with your hardware manufacturer on this). If this applies to you, now you may have that justification you were looking for on ordering that new server.

You may have had no reason to upgrade your operating system before now, but to run TFS you need to have a 64-bit server. Running TFS brings the perfect justification for upgrading your OS!)

Another question I'm getting these days on just about everything is if this (Team Foundation Server 2015 in this case) will support a Server Core installation. It will not. (More information on the Core Installation Option is at http://technet.microsoft.com/en-us/library/cc771345(v=ws.10).aspx.) Just not enough of what TFS needs with these options.

Installation Checklist

Here is a checklist to make sure that you have the basic information to begin. Please refer back to Table 1-1 in future chapters, because you'll be reusing the information here in most chapters.

Table 1-1. *Team Foundation Server 2015 Installation and Configuration Checklist*

Details	Parameters for Installation
Server names for each server involved:	
• Team Foundation 2015 (or the old Team Foundation Server if you are upgrading, and the new server)	☑ TFS Server ☑ Active Directory Domain
• Active Directory Domain / Domain Controller	☑ Domain Controller
• SQL Server (if yours is separate)	☑ SQL Server
• SQL Reporting Services Server (if yours is separate)	☑ SQL Reporting Services Server
• SharePoint Server (if yours is separate)	☑ SharePoint Server
See the "Active Directory" and "Supported Operating System Requirements" sections in this chapter for additional requirements for this environment. If your planned systems don't meet the specifications, go no further until you correct it.	

(continued)

Table 1-1. (*continued*)

Details	Parameters for Installation
Service account names and login information. You'll want this information handy throughout the tasks in this book. If you are creating these, see the "Accounts and Permissions" section in this chapter as well to make sure that you have the permissions set correctly. In a simple single server environment you may choose to use a single account for this, TFSSERVICE for instance.	☑ TFSREPORTS ☑ TFSSEVICE ☑ TFSBUILD ☑ TFSPROXY ☑ WSSSERVICE ☑ SQLSERVICE

You will need these basic accounts for installation and operation (see the "Accounts and Permissions" section). A common question I get is, "Do I need to actually name my accounts this?" You don't. But if you do, it will make your life easier since this is how they are referred to in most Microsoft documentation and this book. But if you don't, here is a handy place to list the equivalents:
 	
     TFSREPORTS – reporting reader account
 	
     TFSSEVICE – the server service
 	
     TFSBUILD – for the build service
 	
     TFSPROXY – for the proxy service
 	
 And you'll need these for the other supporting software (see the "Accounts and Permissions" section, but these are generally user accounts):
 	
     WSSSERVICE – for SharePoint
 	
     SQLSERVICE – for SQL Server	

Visual Studio Team Foundation Server 2015. You'll need this later on during the installation. For now, just locate the Team Foundation Server 2015 DVD or ISO file from MSDN.	☑ Installation Media / ISO

Accounts and Permissions

You will need a number of accounts for installing and running Team Foundation Server. Since the largest number of issues I get questions on end up being permissions related as a root cause, I'm going to suggest that you read this section carefully, without opting for shortcuts. Also, unless you are working on an upgrade where the accounts have been established and working for a while, I'm going to recommend that you establish new accounts and not reuse old ones, especially if this is an enterprise install.

Why you ask? Well, for one thing, people tend to adjust the security settings and permissions of accounts over time either by accident (i.e., having trouble with getting a service to run and giving it Domain Administrator privileges, and then forgetting to set it back), or if you have an IT security group that scans for privileged accounts and scales them back based on the last login date (I worked for a large defense contractor where that was the norm; caused me days of aggravation). You'll avoid that by starting with new accounts.

Also, no section like this would be complete without a disclaimer: these recommendations should fit *most* situations. If you are building a large scaled-out environment in a really security-strict environment, you will likely need to make some additional adjustments to comply with these rules. Also, the user accounts could be domain (recommended) or local accounts. If you are installing a component in a workgroup, you must use local accounts for user accounts, however. The following names are only suggested. There is no real requirement to use a specific name, but if you do not, be sure to list the one you use since I'll be referring to the suggested name from here on out.

Table 1-2 provides the lists of user and service accounts, including descriptions of what they are.

Table 1-2. *TFS Account Permissions*

Where Used	Recommended Name (you will find Microsoft referring to that name)	Permission Requirements	Notes
Installation/ maintenance user account	TFSADMIN	Full System Administrator permissions on the server(s) for the install.	You will likely get some grief if you are in a big IT shop and request this. However, it is definitely recommended to make the install go smoothly.
Reporting	TFSREPORTS	A user account that has the Allow logon locally permission. You will also see this referred to as the Report Reader account since that is what it does. This should *not* be an administrator account.	You will be prompted for this account during the install. You will not be able to specify a built-in account for the report reader account.
Team Foundation Server	TFSSERVICE	Can use a built-in account or a user account. If you use a user account, it must have the logon as a service permission. If a SharePoint site wasn't installed with Team Foundation Server, you need to add TFSSERVICE to the Farm Administrators group for the SharePoint Central Administration site.	*Do not* use the account that you used to install Team Foundation Server as the account for TFSSERVICE. If this installation will use reports, you need to add TFSSERVICE to the Content Manager role on the server that is running SQL Server Reporting Services. This will default in the installation to the Network Service account. This usually works fine.
Team Foundation Build	TFSBUILD	This can be a built-in or a user account. If it's a user account, make sure it has the logon as a service permission.	
Team Foundation Server Proxy	TFSPROXY	This can be a built-in or a user account. If it's a user account, make sure it has the logon as a service permission.	Only used in a Proxy install, but better to have it ready if you decide to deploy this component.
SharePoint products	WSSSERVICE	Needs to be a user account.	If you install Team Foundation Server with the default options, this will be the same as the report reader account. Note: It is also the identity of the application pool for the SharePoint Central Administration site.
SQL Server	SQLSERVICE	This can be a built-in or a user account. If it's a user account, make sure it has the logon as a service permission.	No particular TFS requirements for this account; just make sure SQL Server is functioning normally for the install.

(continued)

5

Table 1-2. (*continued*)

Where Used	Recommended Name (you will find Microsoft referring to that name)	Permission Requirements	Notes
Release Management Server	RMSERVER	Identity used in Internet Information Service (IIS) for the application pool and the Release Management Monitor Windows service.	This will default in the installation to the Network Service account. This usually works fine.
Release Management Server	DEPLOY	This account is used to configure machines in your environment, so it will need whatever permissions are required to do this. Most of the time it will need to be in the Administrators group.	If this account needs to access builds on the network, make sure it has access to the network drop location that you specified in the build.
Release Management Server (connected to TFS)	RMTFS	This is a TFS user that is a member of the Project Collection Administrators group. Set "Make Requests on Behalf of Others" to Allow.	Not sure what this piece is all about yet? Don't worry, we'll hit it again later, and you might not even need it.

Supported Operating System Requirements

If anything, the supported operating systems got tighter this release with the elimination of some platforms. You can use:

Server operating systems (Server Core installations not supported):

- 64-bit versions of Windows Server 2012 R2 (Essentials, Standard, Datacenter)

- 64-bit versions of Windows Server 2012

- 64-bit versions of Windows Server 2008 R2 (Standard, Enterprise, Datacenter)

- Windows Small Business Server 2011 (Standard, Essentials, Premium Add-On)

For the love of sanity, if you choose to go the SBS route, make sure that you calculate your fully configured SBS server with all its components (Exchange, etc.), and then *add* the Team Foundation Server requirements to those. Better yet, use it in your deployment, but not as a single-server TFS solution.

For installations of TFS or SQL Server with Windows Server 2008 R2, you need .NET Framework 3.5 installed. On Windows Server 2008 R2, you can install .NET Framework 3.5 by using the Add Features Wizard from Server Manager.

Supported client operating system requirements:

- Windows 8.1 (Basic, Professional, Enterprise)

- Windows 8

- Windows 7 (Home Premium, Professional, Enterprise, Ultimate, SP1 minimum)

It's best to use a client OS only as a test install for a proof of concept. You will not be able to install SharePoint, Reporting, or TFSProxy. What does this mean for you? No web site to collaborate, no HTML project reports, and you won't be able to proxy source files. Move to a server OS above for any production use. I always find it amazing when I see questions on "performance issues," and then find someone using a client operating system. Also, the "Standard" install isn't supported on a client OS since it installs SharePoint. Have I talked you out of trying to do this on the cheap with a client OS yet? Very good.

Performance and Planning

Nothing gets more hotly contested in systems engineering circles than performance recommendations. The recommendations in Table 1-3 come directly from Microsoft. They are the *minimum*. Take special note of the new hard disk requirements. Also, the numbers do not include recommendations for SharePoint installed on the same server; those recommendations are in the next section. My notes from my personal experience are in a following note.

Table 1-3. *Scaling and Performance Recommendations*

Number of Users	Role	Configuration	CPU	Memory	Hard Disk
Less than 250 users	TFS Server	Single-server (Team Foundation Server and the Database Engine on the same server).	1 single-core processor at 2.13 GHz	2 GB	1 disk at 7.2k rpm (125 GB)
250 to 500 users	TFS Server	Single-server (Team Foundation Server and the Database Engine on the same server).	1 dual-core processor at 2.13 GHz	4 GB	1 disk at 10k rpm (300 GB)
500 to 2,200 users	TFS Server	Dual-server (Team Foundation Server and the Database Engine on **different** servers).	1 dual-core Intel Xeon processor at 2.13 GHz	4 GB	1 disk at 7.2k rpm (500 GB)
	Database Server	This is for the Database Engine portion with 500 to 2,200 users (for preceding configuration).	1 quad-core Intel Xeon processor at 2.33 GHz	8 GB	SAS disk array at 10k rpm (2 TB)
2,200 to 3,600 users	TFS Server	Dual-server (Team Foundation Server and the Database Engine on **different** servers).	1 quad-core Intel Xeon processor at 2.13 GHz	8 GB	1 disk at 7.2k rpm (500 GB)
	Database Server	This row is for the Database Engine with 2,200 to 3,600 users (for preceding configuration). Performance	2 quad-core Intel Xeon processors at 2.33 GHz	16 GB	SAS disk array at 10k rpm (3 TB)

Hardware

Table 1-3 reviews the general hardware recommendations for Team Foundation Server, broken out by tier or role. These are good starting recommendations, but you need to keep in mind any local considerations that may increase these.

Scaling Tips: One to Many

So you need more performance out of your Team Foundation Server 2015 installation. The first step is to be sure that you meet the minimum requirements in this chapter. Since there are a lot of scenarios here, let's consider this one: you're starting to max out on your single-server installation. The one axiom you will note in any system's performance recommendation chart is that you can never have enough RAM, fast enough processors, or fast enough disk subsystems to support everything on one system. So what, in general, should you scale out to? It really depends on which components in the Team Foundation Server are the heaviest used. For a lot of people, that ends up being the SharePoint Server. After that, move your databases to a separate SQL Server and Reporting Services server.

I covered a very select scenario here, and yours may be different. For more advanced considerations, I highly recommend reading up on Team Foundation Server performance recommendations in the Visual Studio ALM Rangers guide at http://vsarplanningguide.codeplex.com.

SharePoint Requirements

Team Foundation Server 2015 is compatible with both SharePoint 2010 and SharePoint 2013— Foundation, Standard, or Enterprise. If you are planning on using SharePoint products in your configuration (and why wouldn't you want to, really), you'll need to beef up the preceding figures, or alternatively, use another server to host SharePoint. How much beefing up? Let's consider SharePoint Foundation 2013 (which Team Foundation Server installs for you), which needs a 64-bit 4-core CPU and a minimum of 8 GB of RAM. If you install SharePoint 2013 on a server that is also running SQL Server (which is required by the TFS standard configuration), SharePoint recommends that you have 24 GB of system memory; if you have only 8 GB, the Team Foundation installer will throw a warning if you only have 10 GB, but you can finish the install. My advice is that if you intend to install SharePoint on the same server as Team Foundation Server, read up on the requirements at http://technet.microsoft.com/en-us/library/cc262485(v=office.15).aspx. At the very least, plan on adding the memory and disk requirements to your existing minimums for Team Foundation Server.

SQL Server Requirements

With SQL Server you can use SQL Server 2012 or SQL Server 2014, and you have multiple options from there:

- The basic configuration of Team Foundation Server, which comes with SQL Server 2014 Express

- One of the supported editions of SQL Server 2014 (Express, Standard, or Enterprise)

- An existing installation of SQL Server 2012 or SQL Server 2014

In any case, your server needs to fit in one of the following supported configurations detailed in Table 1-4.

Table 1-4. SQL Server Requirements

Requirement	Supported Configuration
Supported editions	SQL Server 2014 Express (limited or no SQL Server high availability support; see note on naming).
	SQL Server 2014 Standard Edition (limited or no SQL Server high availability support).
	SQL Server 2014 Enterprise Edition.
	SQL Server 2012 Express with SP1 (limited or no SQL Server high availability support, see note on naming).
	SQL Server 2012 Standard Edition with SP1 (limited or no SQL Server high availability support); it is strongly recommended to install CU2 or higher on top of SQL Server 2012 SP1.
	SQL Server 2012 Enterprise Edition with SP1; it is strongly recommended to install CU2 or higher on top of SQL Server 2012 SP1 or hotfix KB2793634 minimally.
Required for Team Foundation Server	Database Engine Services (this is your SQL Database). Full-Text and Semantic Extractions for Search.
Required for reporting	Reporting Services—Native. Analysis Services.
Collation settings	Must be accent sensitive.
	Must not be case sensitive.
	Must not be binary.
	Must not be binary – code point.
	For more information, see `http://msdn.microsoft.com/en-us/library/dd578603.aspx`.
Authentication	Windows authentication.
Service account	You can use a domain account or a built-in account.

SQL Server 2014 Performance

TFS 2013 Update 2 adds support for SQL 2014. TFS2015 does as well. The only problem with this is that the hardware requirements to run SQL Server 2014 are much higher than in earlier versions, so if you had a minimal SQL installation prior, SQL Server 2014 might seem like a performance hog. This has caught quite a few people off guard and has generated more than a few support calls. What does this mean for you? Well, if you had your heart set on upgrading to SQL Server 2014 as part of your install, then you may need to do a little more planning and upgrading prior. A good rule of thumb to follow for installations supporting 500+ users is to add 0.4 GB of RAM per collection database. For more detailed information on this issue, or if you have installed SQL 2014 and now have some specific concerns, the Microsoft Knowledge Base article at `http://support.microsoft.com/kb/2953452/en-us` will help.

TFS Express SQL Naming Requirement

One odd thing about using TFS Express is that it only supports SQL Server Express using the default instance name of "SQLExpress". I doubt most people opting for this free edition of TFS will mind, but it's worth pointing out to save headaches later.

SQL Server High Availability Features Supported on Team Foundation Server

So you've heard about the new high availability (HA) features in SQL Server 2012 and SQL Server 2014. Using these requires a Team Foundation Server–specific configuration. The development team tried really hard to make the HA features independent of Team Foundation Server, but some configuration is required, as indicated in Table 1-5.

Table 1-5. *High Availability Feature Support*

SQL Server HA Feature	TFS support	Requires TFS Configuration?
AlwaysOn Failover Cluster Instances (was known as Failover Clustering) / Failover Clustering	Yes	No
AlwaysOn Availability Groups (you can now use more than one in TFS 2015)	Yes	Yes (Must include your TFS_Configuration database and all of the TFS_Collection databases in the group. Select option during install or upgrade on Advanced Wizard only)
SQL Mirroring (Deprecated feature. Available but not recommended. Use AlwaysOn Availability Groups instead)	Yes	No
SQL Replication	No	No
SQL Log Shipping	No	No

The configuration and planning of these advanced features is well beyond the scope of what I can cover here. If you're considering/planning on using these features in a TFS environment, the bottom line is to decide what your tolerance for downtime is, and then plan the HA configuration to support that goal. For further reading, I recommend following this Microsoft link: `http://msdn.microsoft.com/en-us/library/vstudio/jj662725.aspx`).

No Touchy the TFS DB!

Microsoft support is getting a bit testy with users who have scripts, queries, or so forth, that perform read operations on any of the TFS databases, and who then try to get support with it running. So if it does come to a call to support, or if you are going to upgrade an existing installation, I recommend turning this off prior. People have had scripts that read against the TFS DBs for years, mostly to make up for a lack of a management feature or to pull statistics that would be difficult to get at otherwise. I've developed some pretty nifty queries that I use for security checking, for instance. While reads are nondestructive in the general sense, they do put a load on the system and could interfere with debugging tools or an upgrade.

Active Directory

You can install Team Foundation Server on multiple servers if they are all in an Active Directory Domain, and that domain is at the functional level that Team Foundation Server supports. A single server on a workgroup is also supported. You cannot, however, install Team Foundation Server on a server that has domain controllers running Windows NT Server 4.0 (yes, there are still a few around). Table 1-6 shows the functional levels that are *not* supported. All others are considered fair game at this point for TFS 2015.

Table 1-6. *Functional Levels and Active Directory*

Functional Levels for Active Directory Domains	Supported
Windows 2000 mixed-mode domain controllers that are running Windows NT Server 4.0, Windows 2000, Windows Server 2003, and Windows Server 2003 R2.	No
Windows Server 2003 interim-mode domain controllers that are running Windows NT Server 4.0, Windows Server 2003, and Windows Server 2003 R2.	No

Ports

You will likely need to open some ports on your firewall so that Team Foundation Server can communicate with the various interfaces it needs. Table 1-7 shows the default ports that you need to make sure are open. If you have modified your installation, you'll need to verify what these are set to in your environment. This may require you to speak with your IT department if you are in a larger company.

Table 1-7. *Ports*

Service	Default TCP Port	Alternate Port?
SQL Service (Database Engine) Note: This is used for the default instance (the first one); for named instances it uses a dynamically assigned port. Use the SQL Server Configuration Manager to find out.	1433	☑ Alternate Port
SQL Browser Service (Database Engine)	1434	☑ Alternate Port
SQL Server Analysis Services Redirector	2382	☑ Alternate Port
SQL Server Analysis Services	2383	☑ Alternate Port
SQL Server Reporting Services	80	☑ Alternate Port
Report Server (if it's not on the Team Foundation Server)	Windows Management Instrumentation(WMI)	☑ Shared Service Host, ports assigned through DCOM
Default web site (for SharePoint; if you aren't sure, you can use Internet Information Services (IIS) Manager to check)	80	☑ Alternate Port
SharePoint Central Administration (if you aren't sure, just start the app and check; if you need to change it, you will need to do it in both here and in the Bindings for the site in IIS)	17012	☑ Alternate Port
Team Foundation Server	8080	☑ Alternate Port
Team Foundation Server Proxy	8081	☑ Alternate Port
Release Management Server (if you are using this)	1000	☑ Alternate Port

Also, if you are using Windows Firewall, the install process will set the ports for you. If you are using another firewall, you'll need to check the documentation or with your local IT person to figure out how to get these open.

Language Requirements

Team Foundation Server supports the language of the operating system it's put on. However, it can also be installed in English on a non-English system under certain circumstances. Why, you ask? Consider this: you may work with development teams across the world with different servers that you want to include in a scale out deployment. While the operating systems may likely be deployed in the local language, you'll probably want to have a common language on the TFS environment. SharePoint will complicate this a bit. SharePoint must always match whatever language pack is on the TFS server. Table 1-8 shows the allowable combinations of operating system language, TFS, and SharePoint.

Table 1-8. *Language Requirements*

Operating system	Team Foundation Server	SharePoint
English	English	English
English	Language other than English	Language (or language pack) must match Team Foundation Server
Language other than English	English	English (or English-language pack added)
Language other than English	Language must match the operating system	Language (or language pack added) to match Team Foundation Server

Summary

This chapter covered what you need to know to plan a successful Team Foundation Server deployment. Starting with the basic requirements, I provided a list of what you need to run TFS. I also provided a handy checklist. If this is your first time doing a Team Foundation Server deployment, it is highly recommended that you use this checklist. Account permissions were also covered. Please pay particular attention to this; I've had many a customer installation fouled up from not following these requirements. Scaling was also discussed, as well as some specifics on SQL Server requirements, Active Directory, ports, and language requirements.

CHAPTER 2

■ ■ ■

Installing Team Foundation Server

Now comes the fun part! This chapter explores the setup experience and how to manage it. You'll now appreciate the time you spent planning in the first chapter, as you'll be utilizing a lot of the information you gathered. Hopefully, you've followed my advice in the previous chapter and you'll have your checklists together with the required information. If not, no problem. Go back and get it together. I'll wait...

This chapter covers the following:

- Various scenarios you may wish to use and ones that you may not have considered yet

- The general workflow of an install, so you'll know what's coming

- A step-by-step walk-through of a new install

Install Categories

As mentioned in the previous chapter, there are scaling considerations. This is especially true if you are in an existing environment that is maxed out, and this update is part of your plan to add capacity. Most people, however, are looking at single-server environments, or close to that.

In order to satisfy the broadest audience, this is the model that you will follow in this book. If I get into a section where a scaling or high-availability touch point exists, I will mention it in a callout or note toward the end of the chapter. To begin, let's review the main installation types that are available. There are two broad categories, and you need to see which you fall into.

New Install

A new installation is the most straightforward installation type. There are no earlier versions of Team Foundation Server to contend with, and other than the normal prerequisites, you can begin the installation. Here I am going to assume that you are using a single-server configuration and that you haven't chosen to scale the environment to multiple servers (see Chapter 1 for more details on scaling and performance). One important change from versions past: Microsoft is no longer having any of the installation wizards actually install SharePoint Foundation or jump to the SQL Reporting Service Configuration Manager to finish that for you (it will do the integration only), so you'll need to take care of these on your own prior to your install. For instructions on running the SQL Reporting Services Configuration Manager to configure and check SQL, please refer to http://msdn.microsoft.com/en-us/library/Dd578643.aspx. I've also provided a brief review of the process at the end of the of the "Installation Experience" section.

Which Wizard to Use?

Once you get into the install, you'll run into the wizard choice pretty quickly, so it's best to talk about it now. The Team Foundation Server Configuration Center offers you the following installation/configuration choices:

- *Basic*: This will install (as the name implies) just the basic services for running TFS. It will also either install SQL Express, or let you connect to existing SQL Server Standard or Enterprise, but it won't install them for you. You'll get Source Control, Work Item Tracking, and Build Services. You do not get SharePoint or Reporting Services Integration configured, however. All default options are selected for you. It lets you install on a client OS, though, for a really small system.

- *Full Server*: If you need full control over all aspects of the install, this is the choice for you. It only runs on Windows Server OS (so no client OS installs with this one). This wizard is also intended for a single server with the default options. The big difference with this one is that it will also configure SharePoint Foundation 2013, and configure SQL Server Reporting Services. This is the option recommended for most single-server TFS installs, and the one I'll walk through in this book. Additionally, if you need to install or reinstall the Application Tier onto an existing web site, you'll want to use the Application Tier Only wizard instead. The only thing you wouldn't want to use this for is to simply install or reinstall the Application Tier on its own (see next for that) or if you.

- *Application Tier Only*: As the name implies, this is used mainly to install an additional Application Tier (Team Foundation Server) to your existing Team Foundation deployment. You can use it on client and server operating systems. It's also very useful for moving a TFS from one server to another, and for disaster recovery. Don't use this wizard to set up your first Team Foundation Server.

- *Upgrade*: This is the wizard to use to upgrade from an older Team Foundation Server version. It supports both client and server operating systems. Please remember to back up your server prior to starting this wizard. This wizard has come a long way since it was introduced in TFS 2010, but it still never fails to inspire panic, because one of the first things it does is remove the old version, but if this fails, it will not reinstall the old one for you.

Here you will want to install the standard configuration. This makes sense if you want to install Team Foundation Server on a single server with reporting and a team portal. It makes installation much simpler. The workflow you are going to follow here is very simple; I detail it in Figures 2-1 and 2-2 for your reference.

Figure 2-1. *TFS installation workflow*

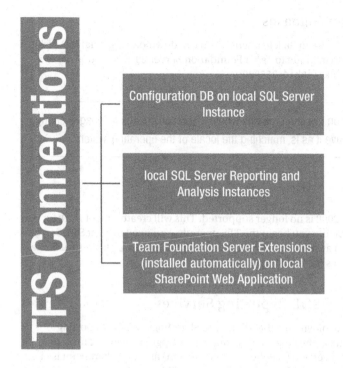

Figure 2-2. *Items configured in a standard single-server installation*

Upgrades

So you aren't going to step through a full upgrade process here; there are just too many variables. And no matter which one I chose, it wouldn't add much value unless it matched your scenario. What would be valuable, though, is reviewing the upgrade requirements, selecting the right options, and reviewing the most common scenarios to ensure a successful upgrade. In a lab environment, you can get away with a lot; however, in a production environment, you need to pay careful attention to the prerequisites and warnings before you begin. You also have some choices to make on what to do with SharePoint and SQL Report Server. Let's dive in.

Prerequisites

I'll review some prerequisites next to avoid roadblocks later during the install, when it can be at least twice as annoying.

Upgrade Paths for TFS

First, you need to see if you can upgrade right to Team Foundation Server 2013, or if you need to take a longer path. So here is a list of the earlier releases you can upgrade directly from:

- Team Foundation Server 2015
- Team Foundation Server 2013
- Team Foundation Server 2012 with Update 4 through Team Foundation Sever 2012
- Team Foundation Server 2010 with Update 1

How About Upgrades from Older Releases?

If you have Team Foundation Server 2008, you are in luck in a sense. You can download a special ISO disk file (vs2012_tfs_enu.iso) that you can use to upgrade to Team Foundation Server 2012. This download is available at http://go.microsoft.com/fwlink?linkid=255990.

■ **Note**   *¿Hablas español?* A frequent question I've seen regards whether you can change languages during the upgrade. No, you cannot. You'll need to leave it as is, matching the locale of the operating system.

SQL Server

As discussed in the first chapter, SQL Server 2008 is no longer supported. This will create a bit of work for you if you are using it; you'll need to upgrade it before you begin the TFS upgrade. You need to be at SQL Server 2012 with cumulative Update 2 at least. If you are considering a jump to SQL Server 2014, please review the system requirements on that carefully since it's quite a jump from SQL 2012.

The Trouble with SharePoint and SQL Reporting Services

I haven't hit many Team Foundation Server deployments that didn't use SharePoint or SQL Reporting Services, and more than likely, both. If you are going to keep these during the upgrade, you just need to make sure that the SQL Server is at the correct version (see the previous section) and that SharePoint is at the correct version, and if so, then you are good to go. SharePoint Services 3.0 and Microsoft Office SharePoint Server 2007 are no longer supported, so you need to stop now to upgrade those, if necessary.

Is it possible for you to skip installing SharePoint and SQL Reporting Services for now and do it later? Not easily, so it's best to take care of that now if they are part of your installation plan. The primary reason is because one of the things that the upgrade wizard does is reconnect all those links to your projects and reports, and doing that manually later would be a real pain; so best to tackle it now.

TFS Upgrade Scenarios

There are three choices for an upgrade path, which is similar to an installation except that the path is more or less chosen for you depending on the environment that the upgrade wizard discovers. Some of the preparation steps are different, however, depending on the scenario that you are in; thus, it's good to understand the differences so that you know where you are going and what is expected.

Back Up!

Make sure that you get a clean TFS backup of all databases and the system itself. This is critical should something go wrong, even as part of an upgrade scenario. What is a "clean" backup of a TFS database? It is a backup that uses transaction marking, as specified in the MSDN article at http://msdn.microsoft.com/en-us/library/ms253070.aspx. Alternatively, if you have a current TFS2012 or later installation, there is a wizard to perform this step for you in the TFS Administrator Console at https://msdn.microsoft.com/en-us/library/hh561429(v=vs.120).aspx. Note these haven't been updated for TFS 2015 as of this writing, but the information still applies.

If you are starting back even further, you should check out my blog entry at www.thecto.org/blogengine/post.aspx?id=5a473b34-9def-4643-b95e-4491139979cf.

TFS Basic or Express Upgrades

The following steps are for upgrading a minimal installation of Team Foundation Server. No SharePoint or Reporting. If either of these are part of your configuration, you need to look at the Standard or Advanced scenario instead.

1. Check the requirements laid out in Chapter 1 of this book. You'll need to have the account names used originally. TFS defaults to using the Network Service, which is usually fine, but you can utilize whatever account was used originally as well.

2. Back up! Make sure that you get a clean TFS backup (see previous note) of the complete system, just in case. This is a good practice with any major system change.

3. Update the system to the latest service packs. Specifically, this is for SQL Express. The easiest way is to go to Windows Update on your TFS system. You may need to reboot after updating, as is usual with some updates.

4. Uninstall TFS if you have TFS 2010 installed. If you are lucky enough to have TFS 2012, you can move to the next step.

5. Upgrade TFS. This is the part that you were waiting for! Locate your media or ISO file, and then select the TFS server installer, `tfs_server.exe`, as shown in Figure 2-3. Upgrade from the Configuration Center menu, as depicted in Figure 2-4.

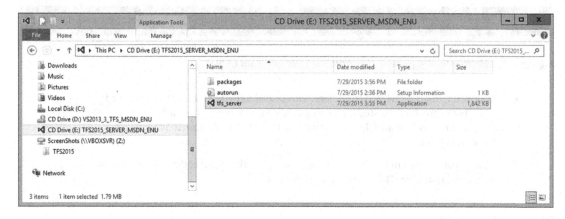

Figure 2-3. *Select the TFS installer*

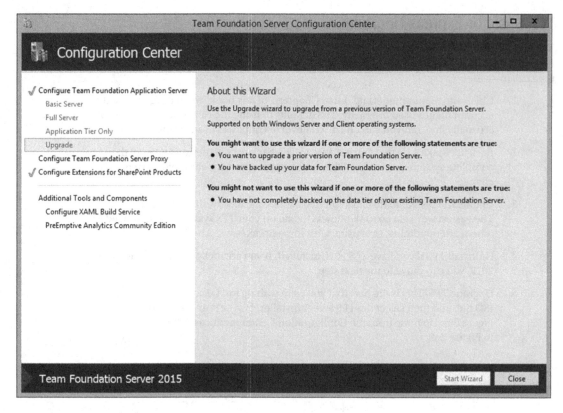

Figure 2-4. *Selecting the Upgrade option from the Configuration Center*

6. Follow the upgrade wizard from here. This is as detailed as I get with the wizard here. For more detailed steps on the upgrade wizard, please consult the TFS Installation Guide available at www.microsoft.com/en-us/download/details. aspx?id=29035.

7. Lastly, you may want to verify that the server is working correctly and/or set up a new build machine. This is covered in Chapter 3.

Standard Upgrade

In the Standard scenario, you are looking at a fairly common situation—an upgrade using the same hardware, or an *in-place upgrade*, as it's commonly called. Here are the installation steps, which are almost identical to the Basic, with the possibility of SharePoint in the mix:

1. Check the requirements as laid out in Chapter 1. You'll need to get the account names used originally. TFS defaults to using the Network Service, which is usually fine, but you can utilize whatever account was used originally.

2. Back up! Make sure that you get a clean TFS backup (see earlier note) of the complete system, just in case. This is a good practice with any major system change.

3. Update the system to the latest service packs. Specifically, this is for SQL. The easiest way is to go to Windows Update on your TFS system if SQL is locally installed. If it isn't, update both servers. You may need to reboot after updating, as is usual with some updates.

4. Uninstall TFS if you have TFS 2010 installed. If you are lucky enough to have TFS 2012, you can move to the next step and retain some app tier settings. Don't worry, this will not delete any TFS databases.

5. If SharePoint is local, then the uninstall wizard will take care of uninstalling the TFS Extensions for SharePoint Server. If not, you will need to uninstall these now on that server.

6. Upgrade TFS. This is the part that you were waiting for! Locate your media or ISO file, and then select the TFS server installer, `tfs_server.exe`. Next, upgrade from the Configuration Center menu. (If you need a visual, please see Figure 2-3).

7. Lastly, you may want to verify that the server is working correctly and/or set up a new build machine. We'll cover some of this in the next chapter.

Advanced Upgrade

Next on the difficulty scale is something referred to as an *advanced upgrade*. The biggest thing here is that you are expected to use different hardware. You may have heard the term *swing migration*. This can be a little nerve-racking, but it's actually ridiculously easy compared to some other centralized version control systems. This is because most of the intelligence in the system is located in the databases, which are portable (with some work). This is how you perform an advanced upgrade:

1. Check the requirements as laid out in Chapter 1. You'll need to have the account names used originally. TFS defaults to using Network Service, which is usually fine, but you can utilize whatever account was used originally.

2. Back up! Make sure that you get a clean TFS backup (see earlier note) of the complete system, just in case. This is a good practice with any major system change.

3. Install SQL Server on your new server. Please review the requirements for SQL for TFS in the previous chapter to make sure that you don't get in a jam mid-upgrade. You are going to install the features that you need (at a minimum). For more details on the install process, please see the beginning of this chapter. The following lists what you'll need to select during the SQL installation process:

    - Database Engine Services (this is your SQL Database)

    - Full-Text and Semantic Extractions for Search

    - Reporting Services – Native

    - Analysis Services

4. Install and set up SharePoint. I'm assuming that you're not skipping the SharePoint products here. You can either use your existing server or set up a new one. The processes are slightly different.

    - For an existing server, you just need to uninstall the existing SharePoint extensions, and then install the new ones, as indicated in previous sections.

- For a new server, it's a little more complex. You'll need to install the TFS Extensions for SharePoint Server first, and then you'll detach the current content database because you are replacing it in the next step.

5. Restore current data. This is actually a pretty cool operation. Basically, you are going to take the existing content and move it to the new servers or location. Yes, I realize that with TFS, the Application Tier isn't there yet. Not to worry. Just restore the databases that you backed up. You can use the TFS backup tool to perform this operation. Further instruction is available at `http://msdn.microsoft.com/en-us/library/jj620932.aspx` if you aren't familiar with it. This tool automatically ensures that you have a clean backup. (Note: This is a TFS2013 link, but the process is the same. No update from Microsoft as of this writing.)

6. Update the system to the latest service packs. Specifically, this is for SQL. The easiest way is to go to Windows Update on your TFS system, if SQL is locally installed. If it isn't, update both servers. You may need to reboot after updating, as is usual with some updates.

7. Uninstall TFS if you have TFS 2010 installed. If you are lucky enough to have TFS 2012 or TFS 2013, you can move to the next step and retain some app tier settings. Don't worry, this will not delete any TFS databases.

8. If SharePoint is local, then the uninstall wizard takes care of uninstalling the TFS Extensions for SharePoint Server. If not, you need to uninstall these now on that server.

9. Upgrade TFS. This is the part that you were waiting for! Locate your media or ISO file, and then select the TFS server installer, `tfs_server.exe`. Next, upgrade from the Configuration Center menu. (If you need a visual, please see Figure 2-3). Please remember to tell the upgrade wizard where your SQL server and your SharePoint server are located.

10. Lastly, you may want to verify that the server is working correctly and/or set up a new build machine. We'll cover this in the next chapter.

Installation Experience

Using the Standard Single Server installation wizard, I'm going to step through the installation process. I'm using this configuration because it's fairly simple for documentation purposes, and one of the more popular layouts for Team Foundation Server.

1. Select the media. Choose the DVD/ISO file for the TFS install, as depicted in Figure 2-5.

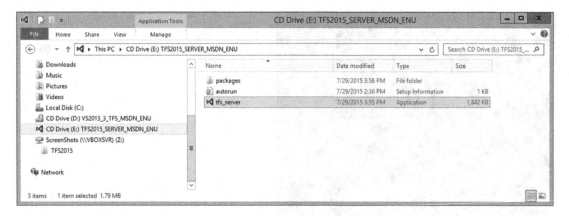

Figure 2-5. *Media selection*

2. Pick a location (most people just leave the default and keep going). Next, accept the license terms (as shown in Figure 2-6) to continue. You'll be presented with a screen similar to Figure 2-7.

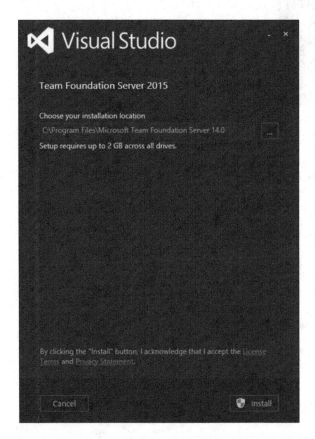

Figure 2-6. *Pick a location for the installation*

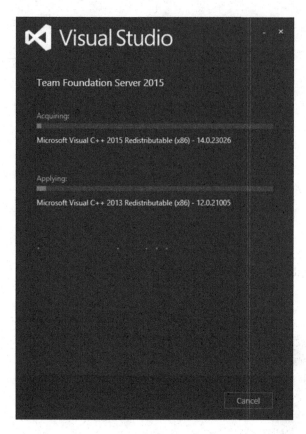

Figure 2-7. *The first progress screen—you are on your way*

3.   Pick a wizard. As I said earlier, you are going to choose the Full Server
     (see Figure 2-8). You'll then be brought to the Full Server Configuration Wizard
     welcome screen. The only option here is to choose if you want to participate in
     the Visual Studio Experience Improvement Program by supplying automatically
     collected information (see Figure 2-9). You can make your own choice on that
     one unless your company has guidelines on this sort of thing. Won't affect the
     configuration either way.

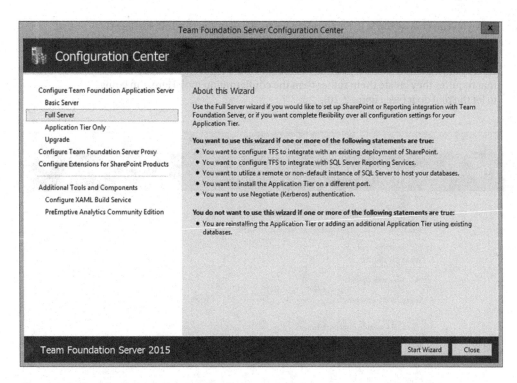

Figure 2-8. *Standard Single Server wizard*

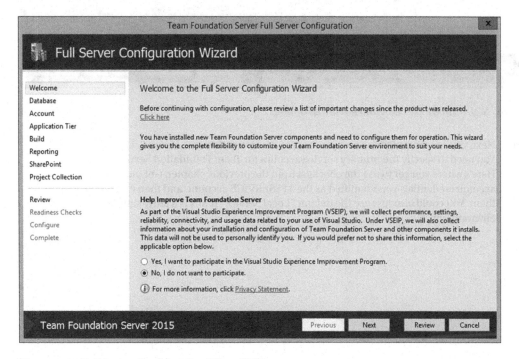

Figure 2-9. *Full Server Configuration Wizard Welcome*

4. Now you can choose the SQL Server Instance to use. You can (and should) test it as I did here. I also expanded but did not use the advanced options. You could use these to use pre-created empty DB's and a Server Database Label. This could be very important in an enterprise environment with a separate database team that requires they create them rather than the configuration tool. Here, I'm going to let the tool do it (see Figure 2-10).

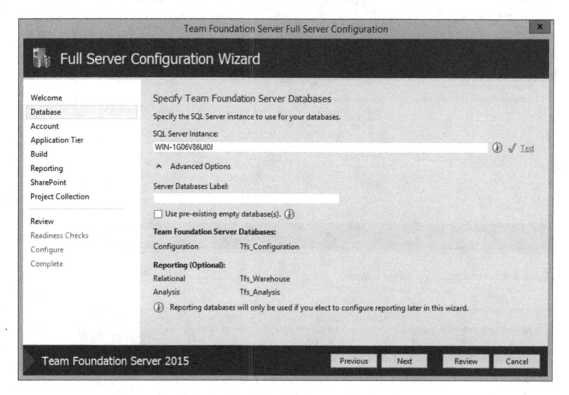

Figure 2-10. *SQL instance selection and advanced options*

5. Next, you are prompted to enter some account information (see Figure 2-11). You need to specify the primary service account for Team Foundation Server. Here's where you get to use the checklist from the previous chapter. Get the account credentials you identified as the TFSSERVICE account, and then enter them. You could also just use the default "Local Service" if this is a fairly simple environment.

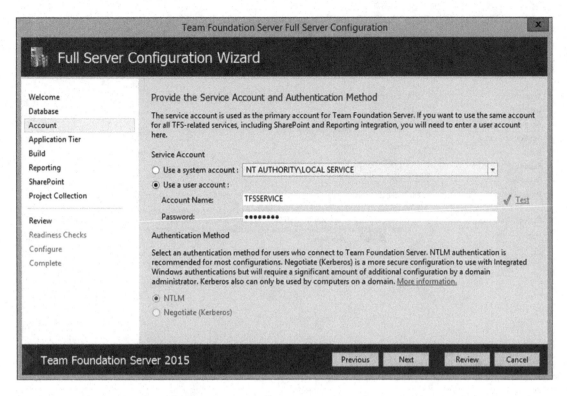

Figure 2-11. *Service account selection*

6. In the next screen (see Figure 2-12), you get to fine-tune your Application Tier settings if you want. You don't need to, all the values you see here were populated by default, but you could adjust the Site, Port, and Virtual Directory. My advice on these is don't get creative and take the defaults unless you can't, makes support afterward easier. For the File Cache you should put this to a non-system drive if possible. Since there is only one on the sample system, I'm going to leave that as default as well. Click Next when ready.

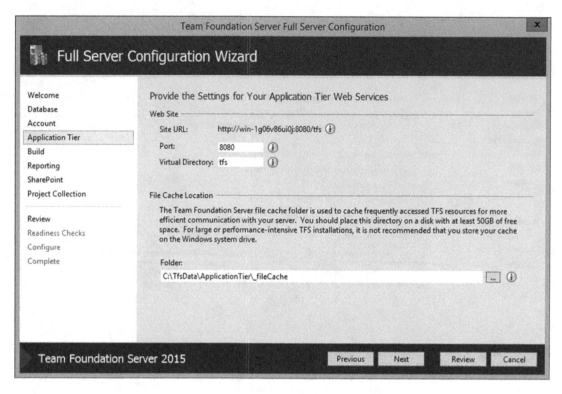

Figure 2-12. *Configuring the Application Tier*

7. The Build Service is the next item (see Figure 2-13). Here you select the service account for the build services and a working folder to perform the builds. This is another place where you can take the defaults and keep moving, but you are going to put the TFSBUILD entry here from the checklist in Chapter 1. I'm going to leave the Auto Start option for the service here, but in a production environment, you'll want to check this.

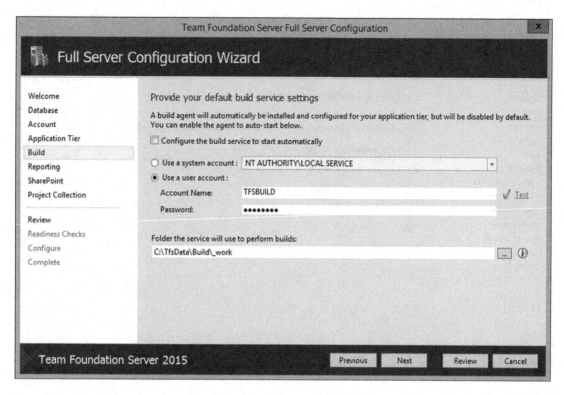

Figure 2-13. *Build Service configuration*

8. Now you need to integrate with reporting services. If this isn't already installed and configured, you'll need to stop here and do that in the SQL Reporting Service Configuration Manager. The option to do this is not checked by default. The installation wizard detects whether or not it is, and alerts you (see Figure 2-14). I'd recommend doing it now if you can. Hit Next.

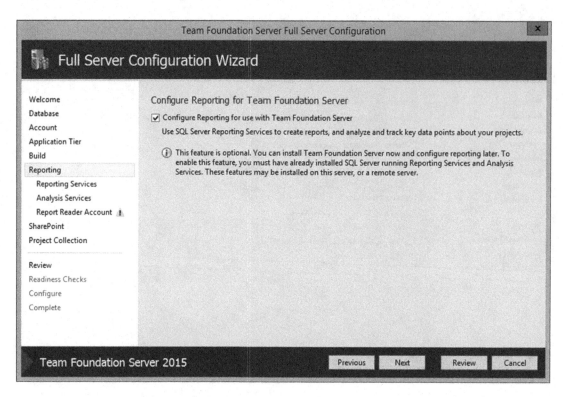

Figure 2-14. *Reporting Services configuration selection*

9. In this next screen, you enter the Reporting Services settings (see Figure 2-15). This is another screen where the defaults are fine for our purposes. You could specify a Reporting Services Instance on a different server, which would be my recommendation for a build-out.

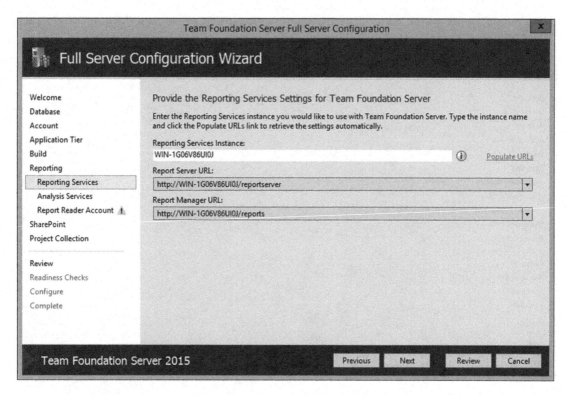

Figure 2-15. *Reporting Services instance selection*

10. Here you simply need to select and verify the Analysis Services. In a larger environment, you would select your Analysis Services Instance on another server. Click Test to verify that the instance is active, as shown in Figure 2-16. Then click Next.

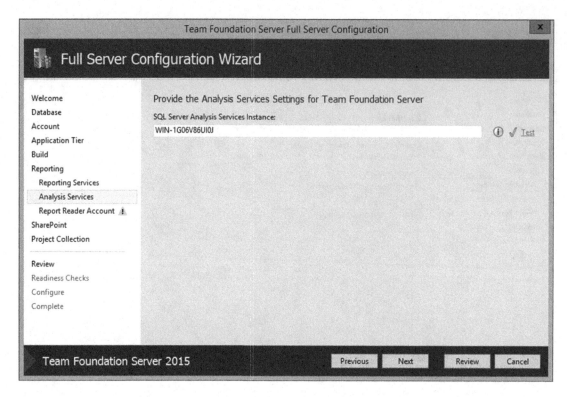

Figure 2-16. Analysis Services selection

11. The last screen for Reporting Services. Here you need an account for the Report Reader. You can get this from your checklist in Chapter 1 on the TFSREPORTS entry. There is no option to use a built-in account (see Figure 2-17).

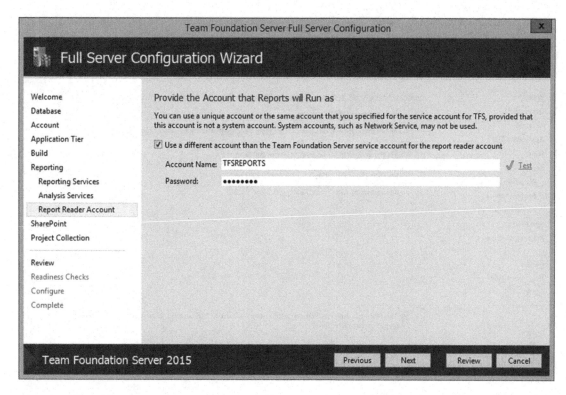

Figure 2-17. *Report Reader Account*

12. On the next screen, you can select to integrate with SharePoint (see Figure 2-18). If the wizard detects SharePoint products, it clicks the box and populates the URLs. Please click Test to ensure that they are valid and then click Next.

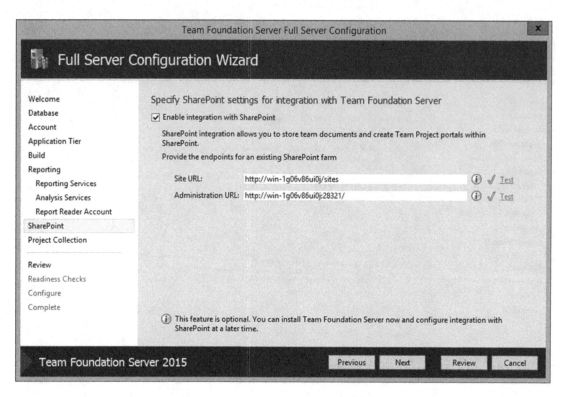

Figure 2-18. SharePoint integration

13. The last item in the wizard that prompts you for data is the Project Collections screen (see Figure 2-19). It is checked to create a default collection; leave this checked and you can alternatively change the name and add a description. You are just going to hit Next here and take the defaults.

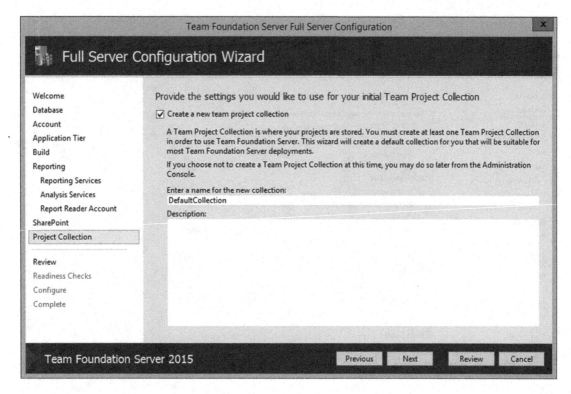

Figure 2-19. *Project Collection*

14. Now you come to the Review screen (see Figure 2-20), where you can double-check your entries one last time. When you are ready, hit Next.

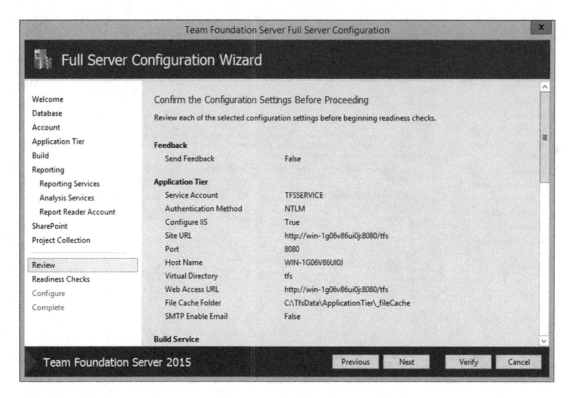

Figure 2-20. *Review screen*

15. On the next screen, you see that the Readiness Checks have completed successfully (see Figure 2-21). You also get a warning if things went wrong, or like in this case, an FYI on some IIS configuration being done on your behalf. It's probably also important to point out that the wizard hasn't affected the system configuration yet, so you could still cancel it without modifying anything. When you click Configure, this next step takes some time.

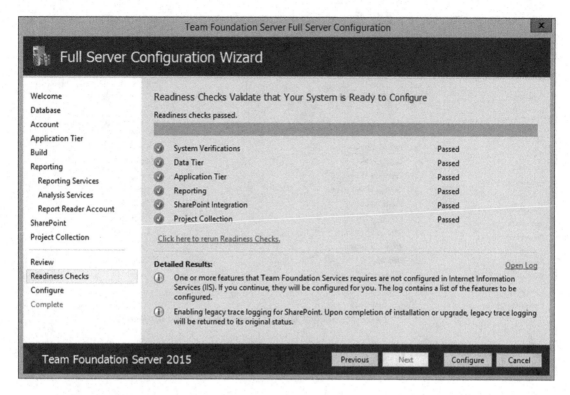

Figure 2-21. *Readiness Checks*

16. The Configure screen (see Figure 2-22) tells you if everything went as planned, and if not, what you need to work on to make it right. If something did go wrong, please review the log link in the next page as well.

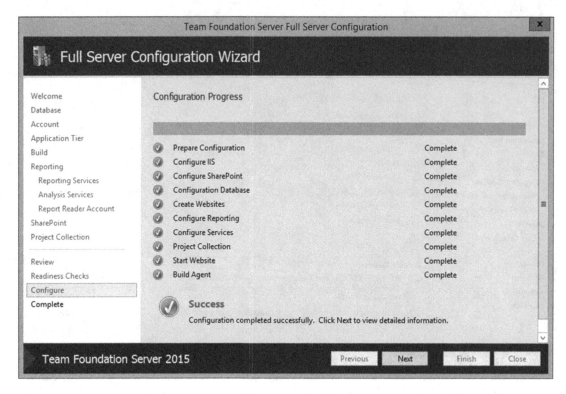

Figure 2-22. *Configuration completed*

17. Finally, you have completed configuration and are presented with the summary screen shown in Figure 2-23. The following are some important things to note on this screen:

- *TFS URL*: http://<server name>:<port>/tfs

- *Detailed Results*: What you find here will vary based on how the configuration went. A few typical items include a note on enabling compression, the port on the firewall that was opened, and a resetting of the Windows service timeout.

- *A link to the configuration log*: It would be a great idea to thoroughly check this log for any errors before continuing.

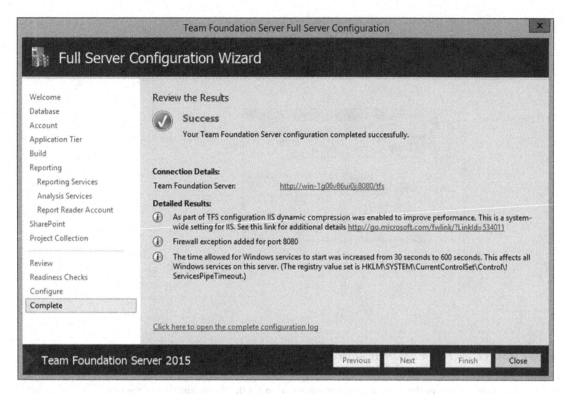

Figure 2-23. *Configuration completed*

SQL Reporting Services Configuration Manager

As promised, I wanted to include some instructions on running the Reporting Services Configuration Manager. If you installed Reporting Services during your SQL install, it should be right on the Start menu. Start ➤ Microsoft SQL Server 2012 ➤ Reporting Services Configuration Manager.

1. In the first screen (see Figure 2-24), you just need to make the connection. This is usually prepopulated, so you just need to click Connect.

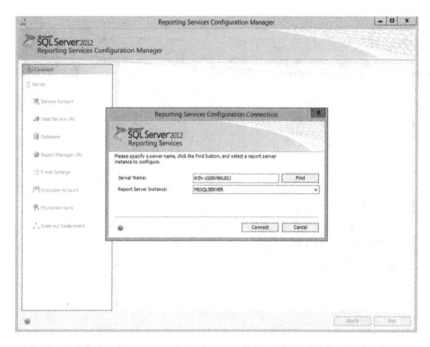

Figure 2-24. *Connect to the Reporting Services instance*

2. Select or enter the service account information for the Reporting Server Service, as depicted in Figure 2-25.

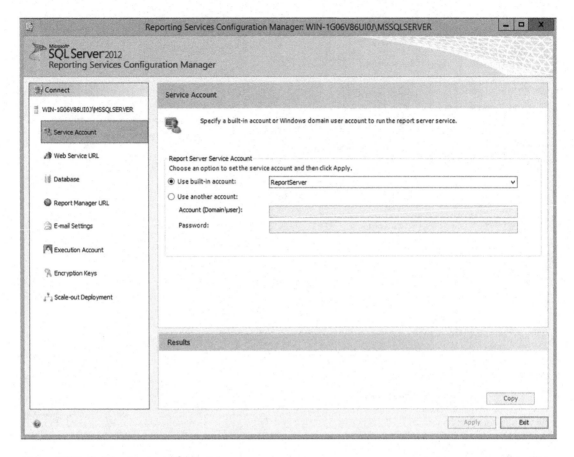

Figure 2-25. *Service Account selection*

3. Next, you need to configure the Web Service URL, as shown in Figure 2-26. If it isn't already configured, you'll be prompted to create it, which is what I did here.

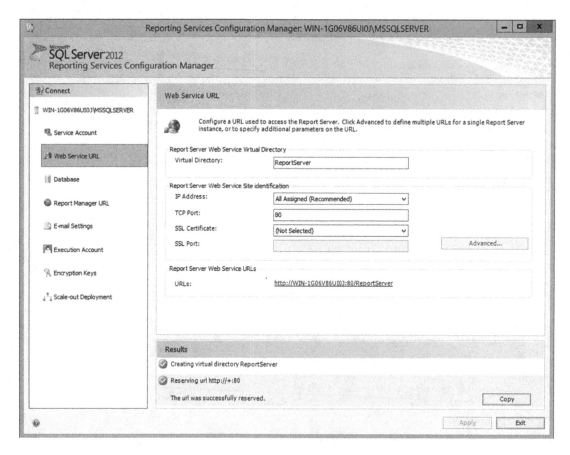

Figure 2-26. *Web Service URL*

4. Next, you'll need to create the DB (if it wasn't done) or connect to it, as I've done in Figure 2-27.

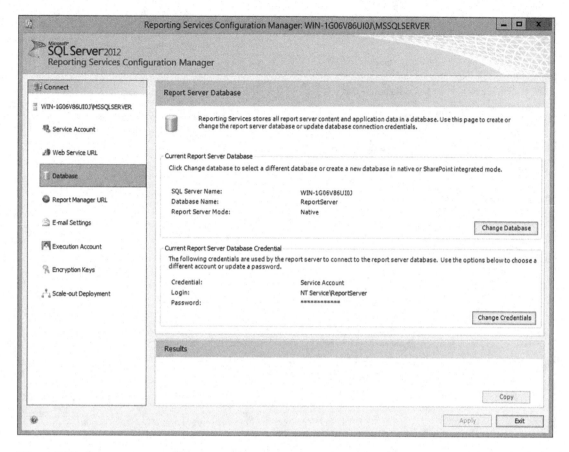

Figure 2-27. *Connect or create DBs*

5. Next, you look at the Report Manager URL in Figure 2-28. Take the defaults here.

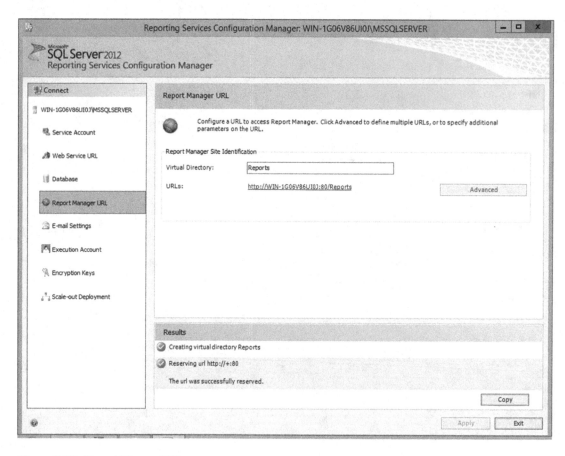

Figure 2-28. *Report Manger URL*

6. Skip email settings for now and go to the Execution Account configuration, as shown in Figure 2-29. You'll want to enter the account you selected for the TFSREPORTS account. Pay careful attention to the format because it's very particular. It must be in a DOMAN\ACCOUNT format, even for a local account; for example, .\TFSREPORTS for a local account. You are going to stop here. You'll skip creating the encryption keys for now, but please put this on your list to do afterward. You will not be able to restore reports without it. You should be able to start or continue your TFS configuration from here.

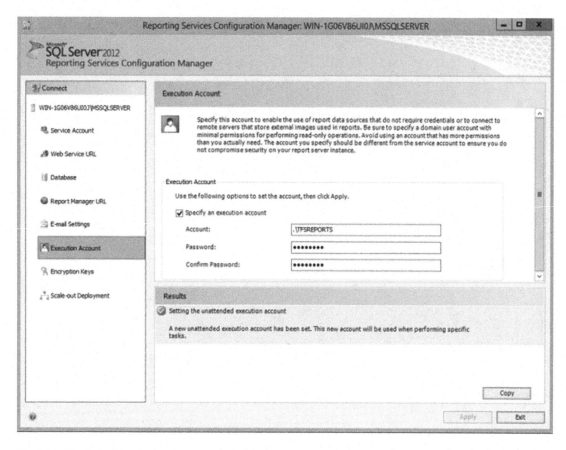

Figure 2-29. *Execution Account*

Summary

This chapter started with an examination of the different installation categories and prerequisites. You also looked at the supported upgrade paths and the common concerns around SharePoint and SQL Server with regard to Team Foundation Server. Last but not least, I walked you through a complete upgrade experience, pointing out what to look for in your installation to help ensure a successful installation.

CHAPTER 3

■ ■ ■

Installation Validation and Security

OK, now that you've successfully installed Team Foundation Server, it's time to validate that it's running. You'll do this by checking some basic things on the system. Then you'll look at TFS security and how to leverage it to save administration.

This chapter covers:

- Validating TFS URLs

- Validating TFS services

- A few words on the installation logs

- Basic setup of the Build Service to validate operation

- A discussion on TFS security and planning

- TFS authentication

Installation Validation

We are all excited to jump in and start using a new set of tools, but first you should probably make sure that the installation went OK; this is fairly simple. You can dive into a few steps that will help you with this. I'll also give a couple of tips for upgrades, since that's fairly specific to your environment.

Validate Team Foundation Server URLs

This one is easy and determines whether a host of services and web sites have been configured correctly. Let's start by looking at the main URLs for the Team Foundation Server (you can get the first one from the Success window from your install, if it is still up; or if you closed it, just follow these next steps).

1. Get the URL. Go to Start menu ➤ Team Foundation Server 2015 ➤ Team Foundation Server Administration Console.

2. Once you have the console open, go to the Application Tier node in the selection tree, as indicated in the screen shown in Figure 3-1. Note the Web Access URL on this page. It will be in the format of `http(s)://<server name>:<port, normally 8080>/tfs`.

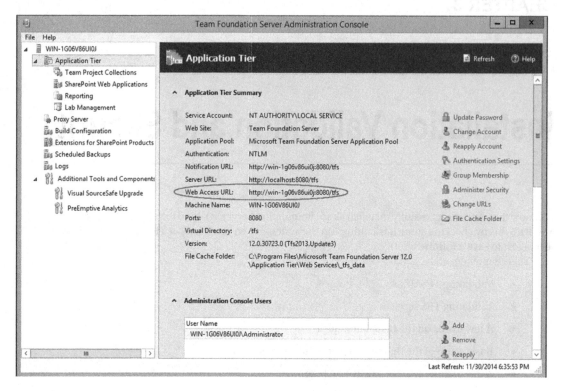

Figure 3-1. *TFS Web Access URL*

3. Now you can check the Web Access services with the URL. (Note that the Server URL is also able to perform this quick test on the local server). Enter that URL in a browser window on the TFS server. You should see a window similar to the one shown in Figure 3-2. Click the Administer panel to open its window (see Figure 3-3). You'll visit this window again later.

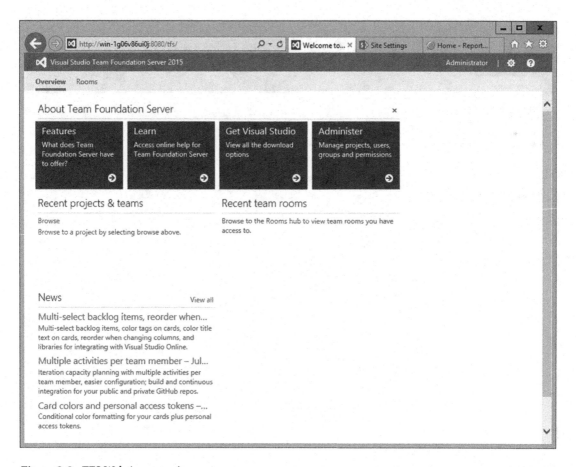

Figure 3-2. *TFS Web Access main page*

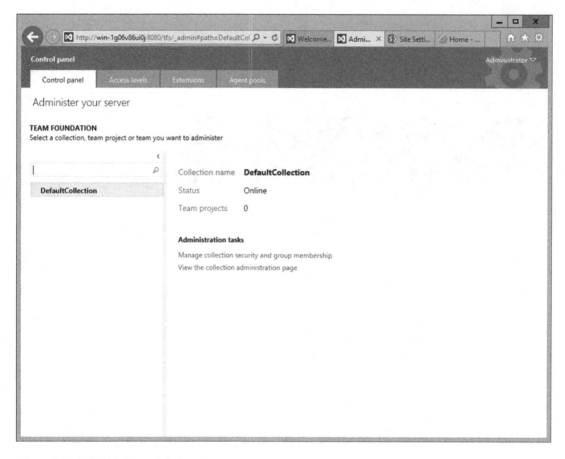

Figure 3-3. *TFS Web Access Admin screen*

Validate TFS Services

Another important step in making sure that your install went smoothly is examining the services installed by Team Foundation Server. Most of the time (actually since TFS 2010), if you make it to the installation confirmation window with a page of green check marks, you are good to go. However, it never hurts to double-check a few things. Since Team Foundation Server runs on the standard Windows Server stack, to do its job, it depends upon a slew of "standard" services and a few specialized ones to be running, including but not limited to the following:

- World Wide Web Publishing Service
- SQL Server (for both TFS and SharePoint)
- SQL Server Reporting Services
- Visual Studio Team Foundation Background Job Agent

These system-level services are to be expected on a Standard Single Server install like the one you performed earlier in this book. If you have another configuration, or a scaled-out deployment, your individual servers would not necessarily run all of these. These are fairly easy to identify in the Service applet; they should be running and set to Automatic startup. There are a bunch of others in a fully configured TFS server as other featured are added (as in the Build Service that you'll check out next), but these are good to start with. An interesting service worth mentioning is the last one on the list. You'll only know something is wrong with the Visual Studio Team Foundation Background Job Agent when things you did in the system don't seem as if they took properly (permissions, for instance), so it's worth an initial check and then monitoring on occasion, because it can be confusing when you set things up properly but they still don't seem to be working, through no fault of your own.

1. Start the Services applet. Go to Start ➤ Administrative Tools ➤ Services.

2. Verify that key services are running and set to Automatic startup, as seen in Figure 3-4.

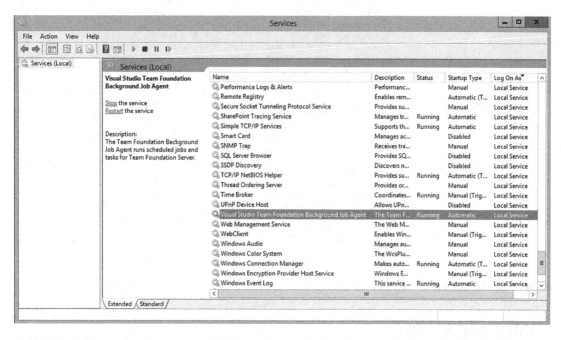

Figure 3-4. *Windows Services applet highlighting the Visual Studio Team Foundation Background Job Agent*

Installation Logs

So I'm sure someone at Microsoft will be upset with me saying this, but the installation logs are of limited usefulness in validating whether an install happened correctly, in the absence of any real errors presented during the installation. Why? There is just too much information in the files that appear to be potential errors, but in reality are just information. However, if you are tracking down a stubborn installation error and can focus on that, or if you are working with Microsoft Technical Support, installation logs can be useful. The location is here:

```
C:\Users\<install account>\AppData\Local\Microsoft\Team Foundation\Setup\Logs
```

So if you were installing under the account TFSADMIN, you would look in:

```
C:\Users\TFSADMIN\AppData\Local\Microsoft\Team Foundation\Setup\Logs
```

For the curious, Figure 3-5 is a typical view of files you might find in this directory. Note the use of the Hidden flag on the View menu in File Explorer. Without selecting it, you'll be staring at an empty directory.

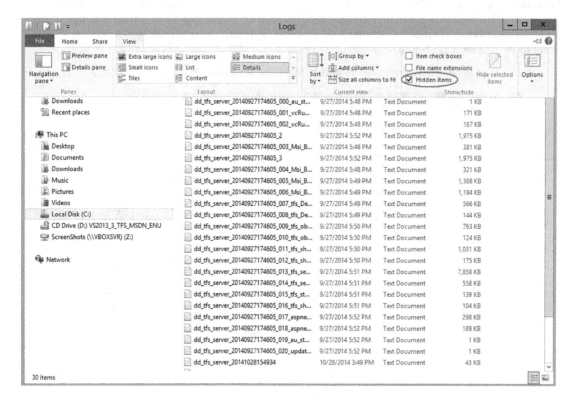

Figure 3-5. *File Explorer in the TFS Logs directory*

XAML Build Service

OK, so the Build Service configuration isn't strictly a validation task, but strays more into configuration. I debated putting it in the last chapter. It is, however, an excellent way to make sure that the system is set up and operating properly, and a good segue into the rest of the configuration tasks you'll need to perform. Microsoft made a departure in this release from putting the "Build Service" node in the Team Foundation Server Administration Console under its own node and now tucks it under the Additional Tools and Components > XAML Build Configuration node. This is also a minor indication of a major build system overhaul that took place including the addition of a Web based UI and expanded third-party capabilities in the new Team Foundation Build 2015. Microsoft now refers to the build features that went into TFS 2010, 2012, 2013, and Visual Studio Online (that were based on the Windows Workflow engine) as XAML Builds. Microsoft has stated that in TFS 2015 and in Visual Studio Online they will continue to support the old XAML Build templates and controllers. What does this mean for us? It means that when we upgrade our on-site servers everything will continue to work as we expect it. The new stuff is not expected to interfere with the old. We'll cover more of the new build system in another section. Here we are just looking to get the XAML stuff up and running to validate our install. Also, companies have invested thousands of hours in setting up their build systems and you'll want to be able to support this "legacy" technology as many people may wish to continue with their investment here before making a switch.

System Requirements

System requirements for the Build Service are the same as the rest of TFS, but it bears mentioning that a few things can bottleneck this service. Sure, a fast CPU and a lot of RAM will have an effect, but from my experience, storage speed seems to have the most dramatic effect overall for Build Services. When you think about it, this makes sense because the XAML build process is indeed writing out files to the disk, which is bound by the speed of the disk subsystem on the server.

XAML Build Service Configuration

Now you get to set up Build Services. This is fairly simple, but I hope my visuals make it even easier. We had you select to install the XAML Build during the TFS configuration so we are already halfway there.

1. Go to Start menu ➤ Team Foundation Server 2015 ➤ Team Foundation Server Administration Console and select the Additional Tools ➤ XAML Build Configuration link as shown in Figure 3-6. This pops up the wizard selection as in Figure 3-7. I will point out that the example you are using here for installing a Build Controller and Agents on the Team Foundation Server Application Tier server is not ideal; if you are planning for a larger, scaled-out environment, you'd want to do this on a dedicated build server for maximum performance. For these examples and smaller environments, however, this way is fine. Click the Start Wizard button on this dialog.

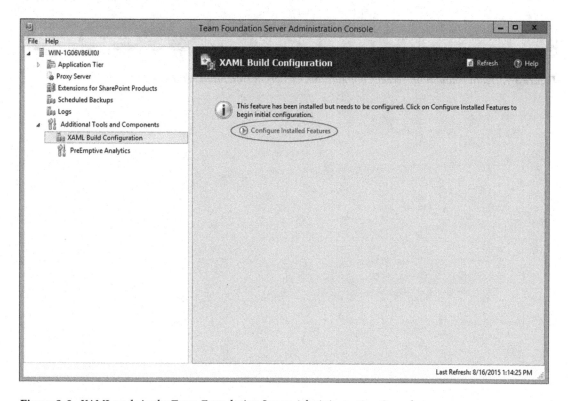

Figure 3-6. *XAML node in the Team Foundation Server Admininstration Console*

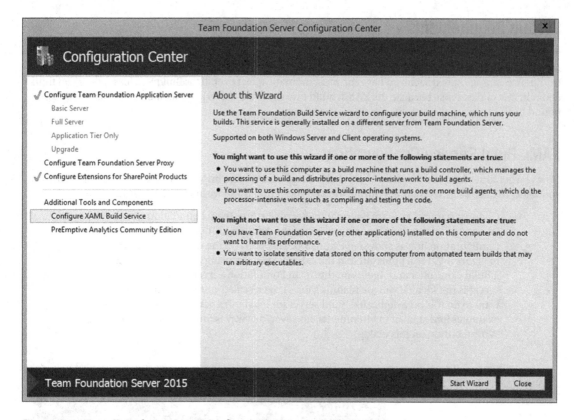

Figure 3-7. *Team Foundation Server Configuration Center—XAML Build Services*

2. Now you need to make a decision on whether you want to participate in the TFS improvement program (see figure 3-8). This will take you to your first real task— selecting a Team Project Collection. The wizard automatically locates the Default Collection on the server you are on, or you can select a different Team Project Collection to work with. Since you haven't the knowledge of Collections and Projects yet, you can just use the default for these purposes. You'll also notice that after the collection selection is made, any existing build controllers and agents, and a total machine count, are displayed (see Figure 3-9). In this case, there should be no others.

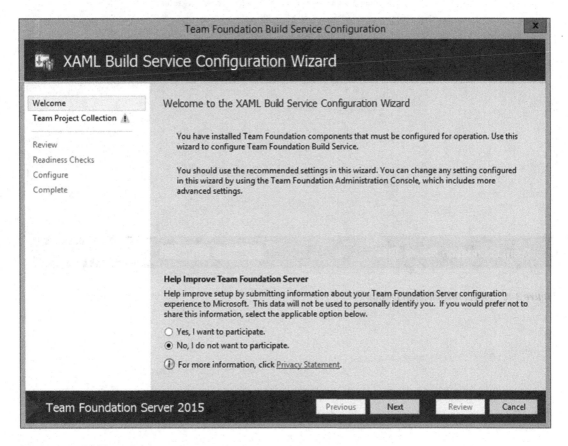

Figure 3-8. *Welcome Screen*

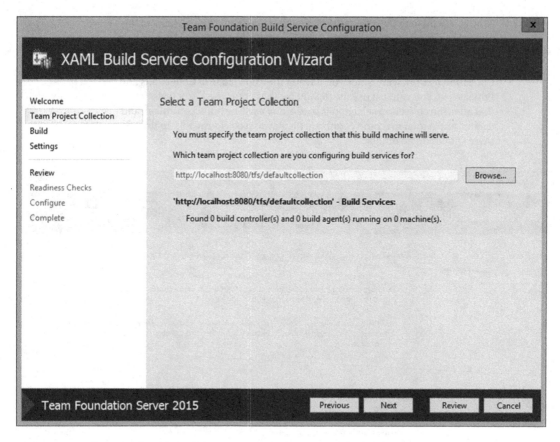

Figure 3-9. Collection Selection Dialog

3. Next Select the number of build agents you want (see Figure 3-10). The default in this dialog is 1, and for our purposes that's fine. A build controller will also be run on this machine. You can select to configure up to four on this dialog, or choose Configure Later to manually configure at a later time. 1 is good for our purposes here.

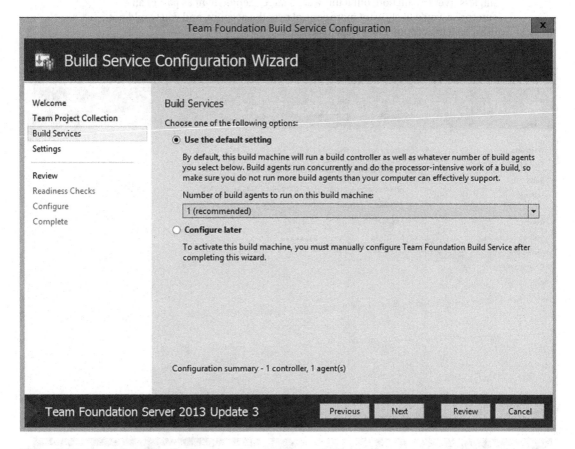

Figure 3-10. *Agent Quantity selection*

4.   Select or enter the security context the build services will run under, as shown in Figure 3-11. This is probably a good time to use the checklist you created in Chapter 1 to look up the TFSBUILD specified account. Remember, if you use a user account, it needs to have Log on As a Service Permission selected. Alternately, you can just use a system account, which is OK for a smaller single-server installation; but if this were a larger deployment as part of an enterprise, you'd likely want more control over the account, and you would not use a system account. Press Next to verify.

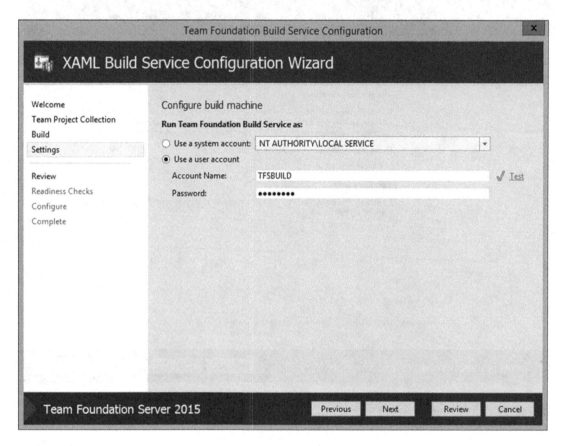

Figure 3-11. *Enter or select a service account for XAML Build Services*

5. Confirm the settings shown in Figure 3-12. Press Next or Verify, and let it rip.

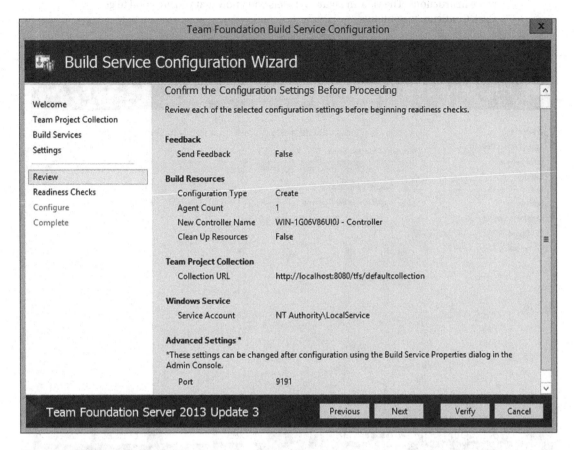

Figure 3-12. Review Settings

6.   Readiness checks. If anything is wrong here, you'll be notified and provided some instructions. The view in Figure 3-13 lets you know that you are good to go. Click Configure to continue.

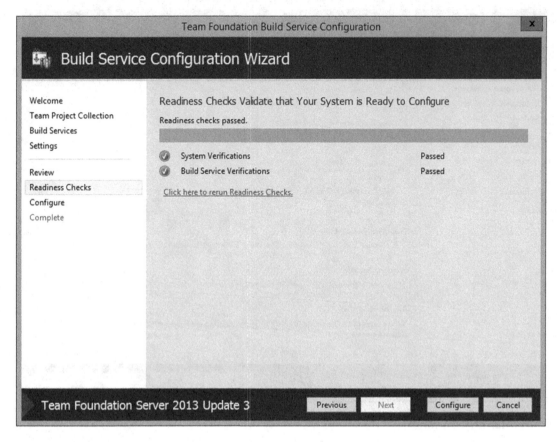

Figure 3-13. *Readiness Checks*

7.   Configuration complete! If everything went correctly, you'll see the screen in Figure 3-14; if not, the exceptions and instructions on how to remediate the issues will be provided. Just click Next here.

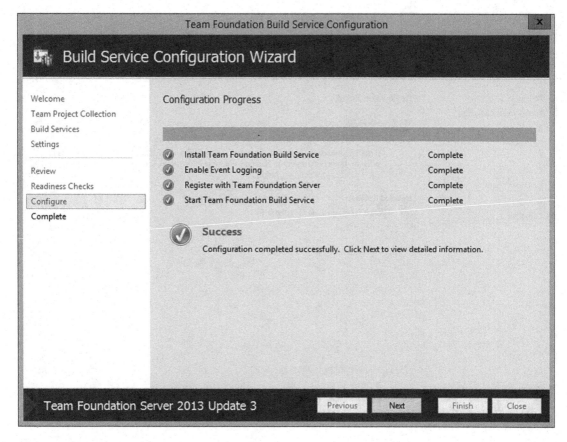

Figure 3-14. Success!

8. Complete. The real completion screen is pictured in Figure 3-15. It lets you know that the configuration worked, and that a firewall exception for port 9191 was added, which only happens if you are using Windows Firewall. If you are using an external firewall, you are on your own with that. You are also presented a handy link for information on working with build agents. I'll cover that in another section. For purposes of validating the install, you are done and you can move forward.

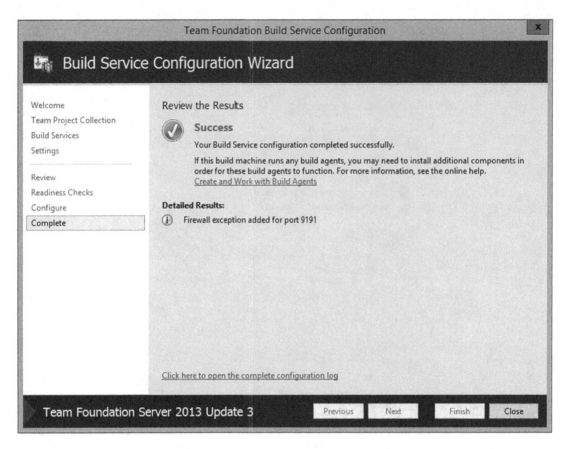

Figure 3-15. *Configuration Complete*

9. The XMAL Build Configuration summary screen. Final words on this. When you close the dialog shown in Figure 3-15 (and its parent), you're presented with the screen you started on (see Figure 3-16), but now rather than just the link to start configuring, you have a nice summary screen that tells you the status of all the controllers and agents in the deployment. Why is this important? Well, if a build agent hangs up, or you want to get a quick glance of your build topology, this is the place to come. I've circled a few things I think you'll want to check on that indicate the current state. You'll revisit this in a detailed section on build, but for now, you've finished what you need to know to validate that the install went well and is ready for the next steps.

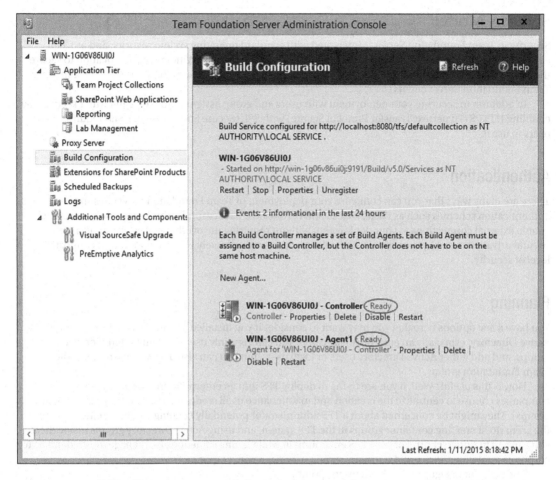

Figure 3-16. *Build Configuration overview dialog in the Team Foundation Server Administration Console*

Team Foundation Server Security

In this section, I'll cover Team Foundation Server security. Like many complex products, there are lots of ways to accomplish the same task; this section covers the most common ones.

You will learn about:

- The Team Foundation Server security model

- Setting up accounts for different roles

- Using Active Directory and user accounts, users and groups, and permissions to secure your Team Foundation Server installation

Team Foundation Server's security model is based on users and groups. You may use the default groups that are built into Team Foundation Server, or create additional ones to customize the model to match the needs of your organization. This allows you to grant permissions to the group without having to set ones for each individual, which could be tedious in a large organization. Likely, you'll want to create ones for specific teams or other organizational units. Hang on before you jump in and start rolling out the new groups, though; there are a couple of things you should consider first.

Security Model

Security in Team Foundation Server is integrated with standard operating system security, and as I said earlier, it is based on users and groups. This means that you are utilizing Windows authentication to secure the connection between members of the solution stack (Visual Studio, Team Foundation Server, and other Team Foundation Server clients).

In addition to securing your deployment with users and group assignments, you can further secure it by enabling HTTPS (Hypertext Transfer Protocol Secure) with SSL (Secure Sockets Layer), and requiring your users to use it.

Authentication

There are many ways that you can configure your deployment of Team Foundation Server to support authentication schemes such as Basic, Digest, and certificates. The reason for this is because you want to enable external connections to your deployment without requiring the overhead of establishing a VPN (virtual private network) connection, which allows you to work remotely while maintaining a comfortable level of security.

Planning

You have a few options here that you may want to consider if you installed TFS into an environment with Active Directory, especially an enterprise-sized one. You can certainly use the Team Foundation Server groups, and add either Active Directory users or local users, but you can also add Active Groups to these Team Foundation groups.

How is this useful? Well, if you are trying to deploy TFS into an enterprise environment, most companies choose to centralize the creation and maintenance of all credentials (accounts, passwords, and groups). They might be concerned about a TFS administrator potentially creating "rouge" credentials. With the scenario of creating container groups in the TFS system, and using Active Directory groups inside these, you can still maintain control of your TFS environment while letting someone else manage the credentials to corporate guidelines. Peace and harmony should now reign with corporate IT.

The diagram in Figure 3-17 illustrates my point.

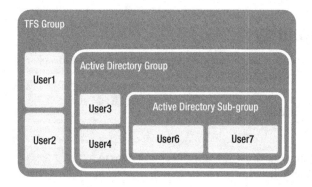

Figure 3-17. *A flexible model diagram showing use of Active Directory groups in TFS*

As I mentioned earlier, TFS's security is based largely on groups and group membership, as it relates to the major parts in TFS. This is an immensely flexible model, and you can really get as complex as you like—or keep it simple, depending on your needs. I'm mentioning this concept now since I will be referring to just the built TFS groups later on, and I don't want you to develop a strategy without this consideration.

Team Foundation Server includes security on every major part of the system, including the following:

- Server level

- Collection level

- Project level

- Area level

- Iteration level

- Version-control level

- Build level

- Lab Management (if you have it)

- Release Management (if you have it)

Let's explore these now so that you have a full understanding of how the users and groups that you add will apply.

Something else that's new and improved this release is Team Web Access. It was always a popular way to get at certain parts of TFS, especially for nonprogrammers. Microsoft has beefed it up again with new controls and the ability to access most areas of the TFS system. I'll be using it whenever possible since it's more universal.

So What Do I Get by Default?

Regardless of what you choose for options, like the process template you select (more on this in a later chapter), there are some default behaviors you need to know about.

Of special consideration is the Contributors group. Every user, by default, is added to this group. Setting permissions on this group will make them active for everyone. This can be useful if you need to quickly set permissions for everyone on the system at once, such as denying access to an on-hold project. However, you also need to avoid being a lazy administrator by setting this group to have every permission available. To do so would create a serious security loophole and you'd drive yourself crazy trying to override it in other groups. Consequently, this is the first place to check for permissions issues that don't seem to make sense.

Default Groups at the Team Project Level

The following are the default groups that you get when you create a Team Project. They all have sets of permissions that are specific to the rolls that are indicated in their names:

- *Project Administrators*: Use this group for exactly what it sounds like—people who need to administer the entire project, including permissions of other team members.

- *Contributors*: I gave this special mention earlier. This is a catch-all for everyone who needs to contribute either source code or work items to the project. Since you may also have project managers and business analysts on the team who need to contribute work items but not source code, I usually create a clone of this group, call it Business, remove the ability to commit source code, and add those roles to it. Do it. You'll thank me later.

- *Readers*: This is kind of self-explanatory by its title, but people in the Readers group only have the ability to read, by default. I've always used this one for documentation people that are saving their work outside the TFS system.

- *Build Administrators*: I'll talk about managing team builds later in the chapter, but this group is handy for people who need to administer the build environment, create and monitor build jobs, and so forth.

- *<Whatever you call the project> Team*: A better group to use rather than Contributors when you want to explicitly set the permissions for your project team.

Securing Team Web Access: Access Levels

Technically, web access is more license management than security, but it is handled via the security tools, so I'll cover it here. The concept with this is fairly simple: you control the features of Team Web Access that each user can use by membership in this group. You'll explore these features in other chapters, but I want to have them listed here for your reference. The Basic is default, by default but you can change that so that new users automatically get another level.

- *Basic (default)*: Will need a TFS client-access license (CAL) or Visual Studio Professional with MSDN subscription to enjoy this access level.

- *Stakeholder*: The only freebee here, no license needed. Good for customers we need to work with but aren't expected to use source control, etc.

- *Advanced*: Will need an MSDN subscription for this group. Either Visual Studio Ultimate with MSDN, Visual Studio Premium with MSDN, MSDN Platforms, or Visual Studio Test Professional with MSDN. As the name implies, all features are accessible to users in this group. This includes everything mentioned in the previous item, plus Request and Manage Feedback, Test Case Management, Team Rooms, and Agile Portfolio Management.

Feature Break Down by Access Level

I compiled this list of features (see Table 3-1) you'll have access to by Access Level to help you plan better. This type of information is always subject to change but as of this writing and release it's accurate.

Table 3-1. *Feature Access by Access Level*

Stakeholder	Basic	Advanced
Gets to use....	Gets to use....	Gets to use....
View My Work Items	View My Work Items	View My Work Items
Standard Features	Standard Features	Standard Features
Agile boards	Agile boards	Agile boards
	Basic backlog and sprint planning tools	Basic backlog and sprint planning tools
	Chart Viewing	Request and Manage Feedback
	Code	Web-based Test Execution
	Build	Web-based Test Case Management
	Administer account	Team rooms
	Advanced home page	Agile Portfolio Management
	Advanced backlog and sprint planning tools	Chart Viewing
		Chart Authoring
	Web-based Test Execution	Code
	Advanced portfolio management	Build
	Team rooms	Administer account
	Chart Authoring	Advanced home page
	Analyze test results and manage machine groups	Advanced backlog and sprint planning tools
		Advanced portfolio management
		Analyze test results and manage machine groups

Summary

In this chapter, you looked at validating the installation with basic methods, such as testing URLs and services. In addition, you looked at setting up build services to validate the installation. You also examined TFS security and authentication, as well as some ideas on making management a little easier. Now that you are sure the TFS environment is installed and working, you can move forward to configuring other parts of the environment.

CHAPTER 4

■ ■ ■

Managing Collections

This chapter explores collections in Team Foundation server, including their practical usage and management. Now that you have a solid server to work with, you'll also look at other major aspects of managing other big pieces in TFS.

This chapter covers:

- An overview of collections and projects

- Setting up and managing collections

- Moving and splitting collections

Collections and Projects Overview

The two major "containers" in TFS are collections and projects (more on these in the next chapter). Whereas team projects (not to be confused with Visual Studio projects) have been around for a while, collections are a relatively recent feature (circa TFS 2010). To give some context, I'll reintroduce the architecture drawing from the first chapter. Specifically, I want to point out that TFS collections exist in the data tier of TFS, as pictured in Figure 4-1.

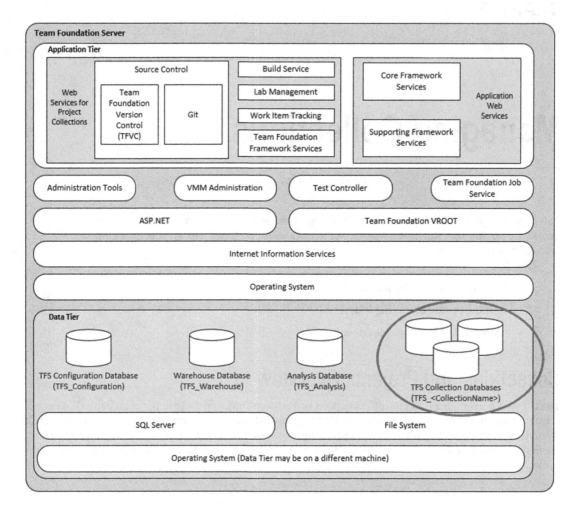

Figure 4-1. *Team Foundation Server architecture: TFS collection databases are circled*

So why am I pointing this out? Just in case someone in IT is curious when new databases start showing up in your data tier; but it's also something you need to keep in mind for backup if you're only set up to back up a fixed set of databases. If you are in an enterprise environment, this is definitely something you'll want to coordinate with your IT group before you assume your recovery after a disaster will be complete.

What Are They?

Collections are logical (or they should be) groupings of team projects and any resources those team projects may need. Team projects, on the other hand, serve as containers for your source control, team builds, work items, documents, and reports that are in Team Foundation Server. I'll cover setting them up a little later in this chapter, but it would be good to put their usage in a little context.

Collection Naming Convention

The naming conventions for collections are pretty simple. They follow the form of TFS_<CollectionName>. You cannot use spaces or reserved characters when you create one (later in this section). Your default collection would be named TFS_DefaultCollection, for instance. The following are a number of naming convention restrictions that you'll want to keep in mind:

- Length: 64 Unicode characters

- Uniqueness: It can't be identical to any other collection name in your Team Foundation Server deployment. If you're using SharePoint or SQL Server Reporting Services, it can't be identical to the name and full path of an existing SharePoint site, report server, or Reporting Services web site.

- Special characters:

  - No Unicode control characters or surrogate characters

  - None of these printable characters: / : \ ~ & % ; @ ' " ? < > | # $ * } { , + = [ ]

  - No ellipsis (...) or double periods (..)

  - It can't start with an underscore (_)

  - It can't start or end with a period (.)

- Reserved names: It can't be a system-reserved name, such as PRN, COM1, COM2, COM3, COM4, COM5, COM6, COM7, COM8, COM9, COM10, LPT1, LPT2, LPT3, LPT4, LPT5, LPT6, LPT7, LPT8, LPT9, NUL, CON, AUX, Web, or WEB

Setting Up and Managing Team Project Collections

Depending on your idea of fun, it's time for another fun part. I'll begin with a few words on where to find collections, move on to how to create a new collection, and then discuss some management and usage ideas.

The primary tools you'll use are the Team Foundation Server administration console, and then later you'll use Visual Studio.

Team Project Collections

Collections are objects that you can see in the data tier. Their database contains a set of projects. So why do we need them? They serve as another container hierarchy level with their own security levels to achieve a more granular level of control over the said set of projects.

Team project collections give you a whole other level of control and scalability in your deployment. Reference the data tier in Figure 4-1 and consider that the collection exists at a database level. What benefit is that? Well, for example, let's say that all team projects for a certain product that your company makes (e.g., commercial software) is placed in a collection. If you decide to move that product to another team or to outsource it, you can easily move it to a different server's data tier. Also, it provides you with yet another level of security abstraction. Very handy if your corporate or government security guidelines call for separate storage of source code on sensitive development efforts. By default, you get one called *Default Collection*, so I'm guessing that you can have one named more appropriately.

Manage Team Project Collections

To manage team project collections, you use the Team Foundation Server administration console. You'll use it frequently, so you may want to pin it to your Start menu if you haven't already done so. It's also worth mentioning that if you are not using the account you used to install TFS, you need to be added to the Team Foundation Administrators group at the server level. Let's go over some common operations that you'll be doing with collections. There are a number of maintenance operations that you can do from this screen as well. I'll cover those in a minute.

Creating a Collection

1. Go to the Start menu and select Team Foundation Server 2015 ➤ Team Foundation Server Administration Console.

2. Navigate to the server and select Application Tier ➤ Team Project Collections (see Figure 4-2).

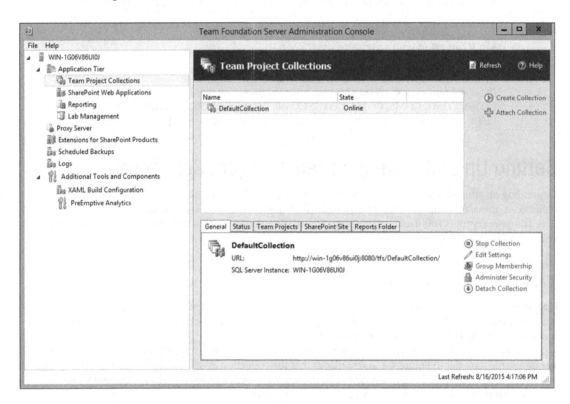

Figure 4-2. Team Foundation Server Administration Console

3. From here, select the **Create Collection** button in the upper-right section of the screen. This will bring you to Create Team Project Dialog wizard that you see in Figure 4-3. It walks you right through the process of creating a new collection. Enter the name of the new collection (keep in mind the naming conventions discussed previously) and a description. The description, although not mandatory, will make your life easier when you are wondering why you ever created the collection in the first place. In this example, you are using **ImportantProjects** as a name. You may, of course, enter one that makes sense for you. Click the **Next** button when you are ready.

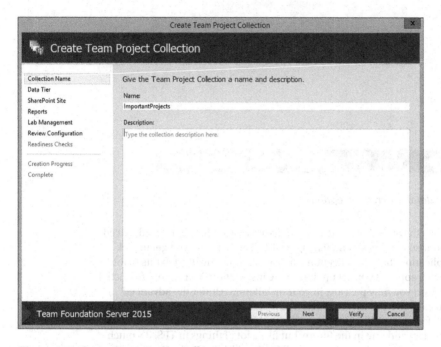

Figure 4-3. *Create Team Project Collection start screen*

4. Now you have the option to let the wizard create a database for you on the default SQL Server instance, or you can specify an existing empty database (see Figure 4-4). Note that you can type in a new SQL Server instance here as well. So why is specifying an existing database necessary? In large enterprise environments, the ability to create a new database is largely locked down, so your only option is to have one created for you and use it. Luckily, TFS supports this. You are going to take the defaults and keep moving. Hit Next when you're ready.

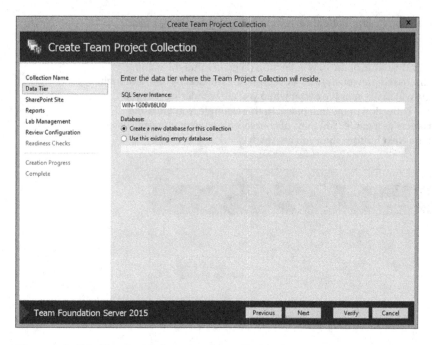

Figure 4-4. *Selecting the database creation option*

5. Next you select the SharePoint Site options. (Note that I expanded the advanced options, if your screen doesn't match Figure 4-5 exactly.) Here you get to pick the web application that the collection will use. It automatically defaults to the SharePoint web app that you set up during the installation. You are not restricted to that, however; you may pick any in your installation. Under the advanced options, you can have the wizard create a new SharePoint site for the collection (this is the default), supply a path to an existing site, or you may not create one at this time. You can add one in the future, but like a lot of things in TFS, it's much easier to do it now. I'm going to leave the defaults in this example. Once you've made your selections, click **Next**.

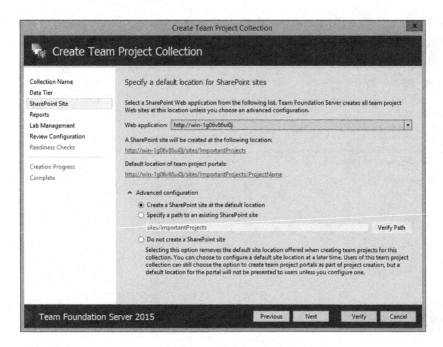

Figure 4-5. Setting SharePoint options

6. Now you'll look at the reports location for the collection. Looking at Figure 4-6, you can probably tell that you have limited options; but you could change the folder path from the default pattern of **/TfsReports/<Collection Name>**. So in this case, you'll take the default **/TfsReports/ImportantProjects**. Alternatively, you could disable report writing by choosing the **Do not create a report folder** option. Like I mentioned in a previous step, you can go back, but it's much easier to create it now. A lot of these options are intended to help an enterprise user adapt to a much stricter environment. If that's not you, count your blessings and click **Next**.

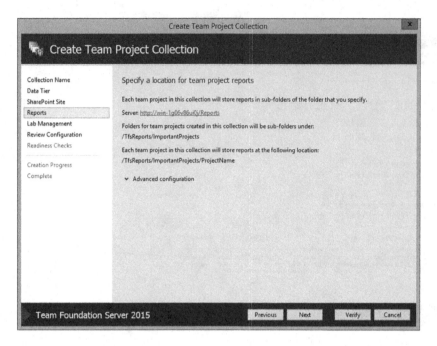

Figure 4-6. Reports location

7. So as you can see in Figure 4-7, you haven't set up Lab Management yet. We aren't going to cover that here, and I want to keep this chapter on track. Click **Next**, and you are on to the review.

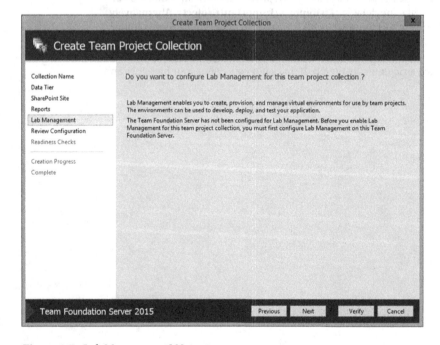

Figure 4-7. Lab Management? Not yet

8. Review the configuration. You shouldn't see any surprises in Figure 4-8, but if you do, it's a good time to back up and correct them. If everything is good, hit **Verify**. You are now moving on to Readiness Checks.

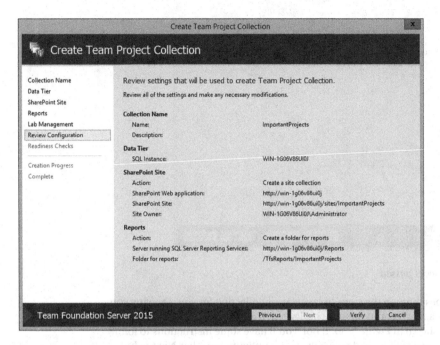

Figure 4-8. *Review your configuration*

9. If everything was successful, you passed the readiness checks and you see the screen shown in Figure 4-9. If did not go successfully, you will get a set of instructions to follow up on. Click **Create** to proceed.

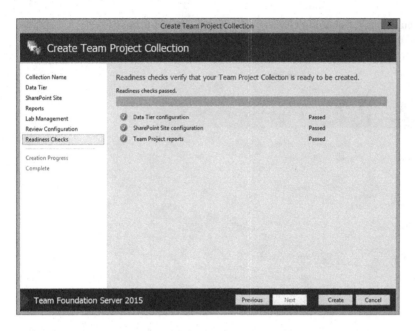

Figure 4-9. *Readiness checks passed*

10. Next, TFS goes through the steps to create your collection for you, showing you the progress as each component is configured. If all goes well, you'll see a screen like the one shown in Figure 4-10. If not, you'll have some instructions to follow up on. When you are finished reviewing your configuration, click **Next** to be brought to the completion screen.

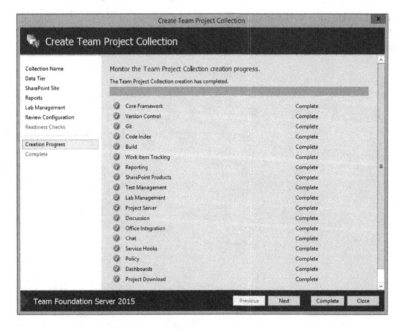

Figure 4-10. *Configuration success*

11. If everything completed successfully, you'll get a screen similar to the one shown in Figure 4-11. Note that there is a link to the log that was created during this process. Of course, if something went wrong, you'll have some things to follow up on. Note that there is a link to the log that was created during this process.

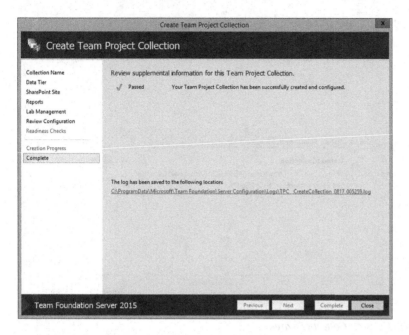

Figure 4-11. *Completion*

Moving a Collection

During a TFS server's life cycle, you will likely exceed its storage capacity, or your organization's needs may change, requiring you to move your team project collection to a different TFS server. Luckily, this is a fairly straightforward, well-tooled process; you'll walk through it here. There isn't a complete start-to-finish wizard, however, so it's important that the steps you go through next are done completely and in order to conduct a successful move.

A prerequisite I will mention here is on permissions. If this deployment uses SharePoint products, you need to make sure that the account you are using is part of the Farm Administrators group; otherwise, you'll be in for a load of errors when you reattach, and you'll likely have to redo the whole operation. OK, let's begin!

1. Go to the Start menu ➤ Team Foundation Server 2013 ➤ Team Foundation Server Administration Console.

2. Navigate to the server ➤ Application Tier ➤ Team Project Collections (see Figure 4-12).

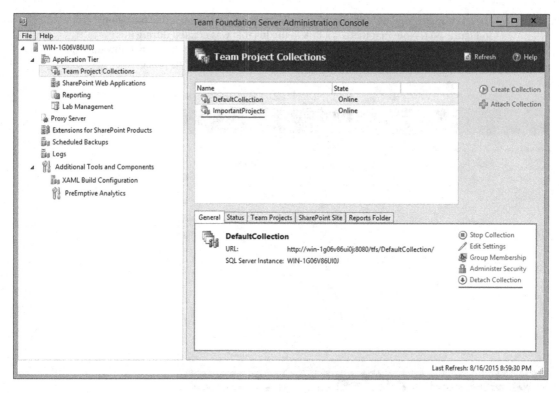

Figure 4-12. *TFS Administration Console, Collections area*

3.   Now you are going to detach the collection. The first step is to actually move it. A word of caution here: once you detach the collection, no one can access it, so it's best to make sure that everyone is ready. In the top panel, select your collection to detach; in this example it's **ImportantProjects**. On the **General** tab, select **Detach Collection as indicated** (see Figure 4-12).

4.   This brings up the Detach Team Project wizard, as seen in Figure 4-13. Here you can enter a servicing message to be displayed to users as they try to connect to the team project collection. A message is a great idea. If you make the message very clear and give users an idea of when they can expect to have the project back online, your local support people will appreciate not having to answer this additional call. Also, this is good time for a backup so we'll do one with the attached link and use the new TFS2015 tool just for that.

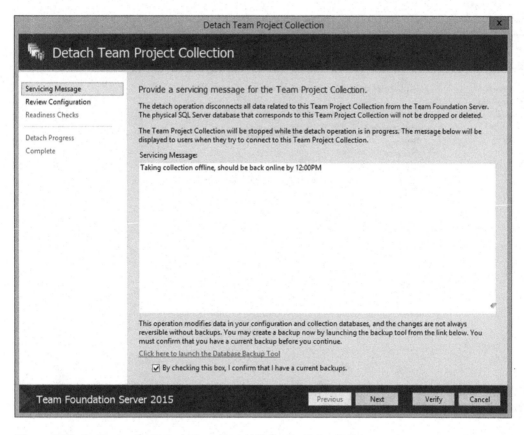

Figure 4-13. *Beginning the Detach Team Project Collection wizard*

5. Next, you review the settings (see Figure 4-14). Click **Verify** when you are ready to proceed to the verification tests (**Next** will be grayed out).

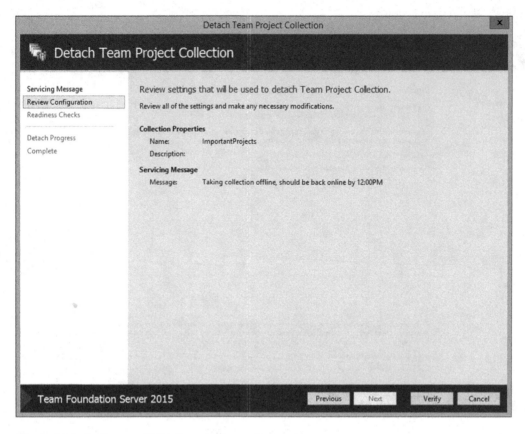

Figure 4-14. *Review your Collection selection and message*

6. Next, you are brought to the verification screen, where hopefully the collection is reported as ready to detach (see Figure 4-15). If not, you are notified about the specific things that you'll need to follow up on. The good news is that this is done prior to attempting to detach, so you have a chance to follow up on any issues before effecting service to your users.

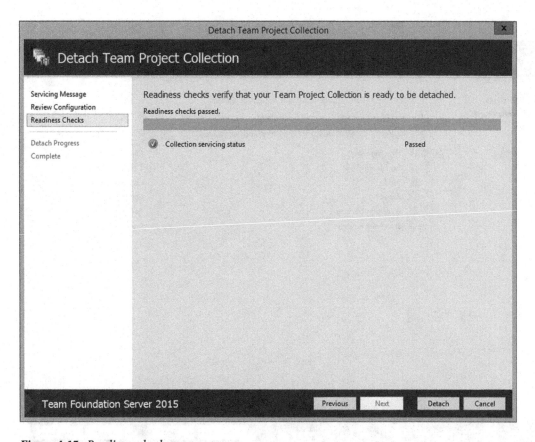

Figure 4-15. Readiness checks screen

7. Click the **Detach** button. Since the readiness checks passed, you get the result you expected. Success! Figure 4-16 shows the different items that were detached and it gives you some indication of progress in a long operation. To finish, click the **Complete** button. You are brought to the final screen in the wizard.

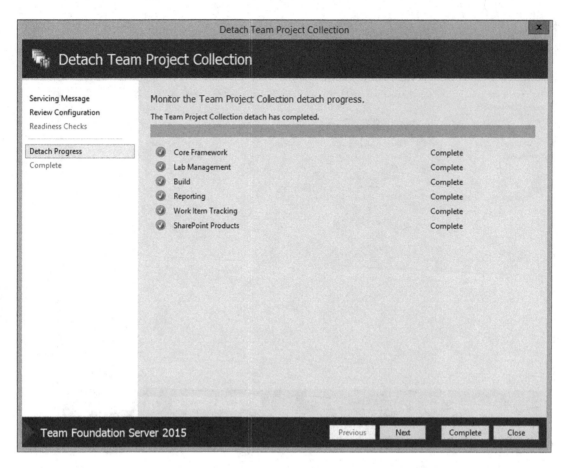

Figure 4-16. *Detaching progress*

8.   Finally, you are done with the detach. You should see a screen with similar to the one shown in Figure 4-17. If something went wrong, you'd be given more information on what to do next. You'd also be given the location of the operation's log in case you do need to follow up on errors. You can click **Close** to go back to the Team Foundation Server administration console.

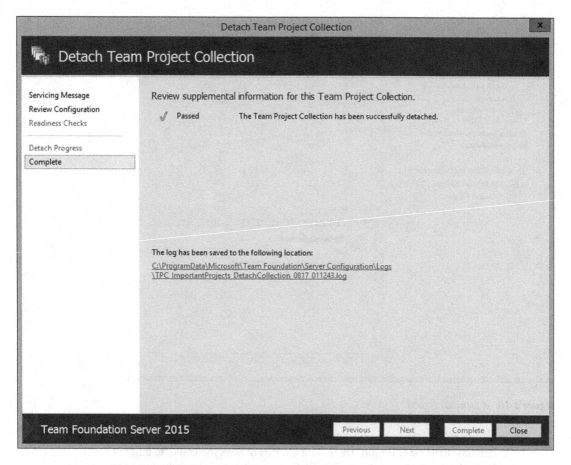

Figure 4-17. *Detachment complete*

9. So now you are back at a familiar screen, the Team Foundation Server Administration Console (see Figure 4-18). At this point, you can move the collection by moving its database file, which is covered next. You can also change your mind and immediately reattach it with the Attach Collection feature.

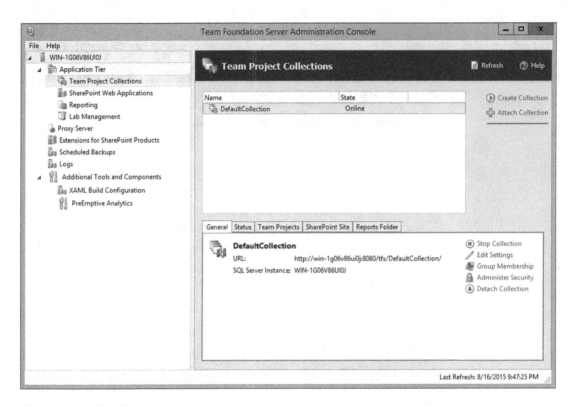

Figure 4-18. *A familiar screen*

10. So now that you have detached the collection, you need to move the collection
database to its new location. There are a number of ways you could do this, but
by far the simplest way is to use the SQL Backup utility. Let's begin by going Start
➤ SQL Server Management Studio. Once there, connect to the SQL server that
houses TFS. Locate your database under Databases ➤ TFS_ImportantProjects
(see Figure 4-19). Right-click this and select Tasks ➤ Backup. From this applet,
ensure that a **Full** backup is selected, and then make note of the file location and
name, as indicated, so that you can easily find it later (if you are doing a manual
move). Hit the **OK** button to back it up. If you need more information on backing
up than I've provided, please refer to your SQL Server documentation. If you used
the tool in the previous steps, you can skip this; you just need to locate the backup.

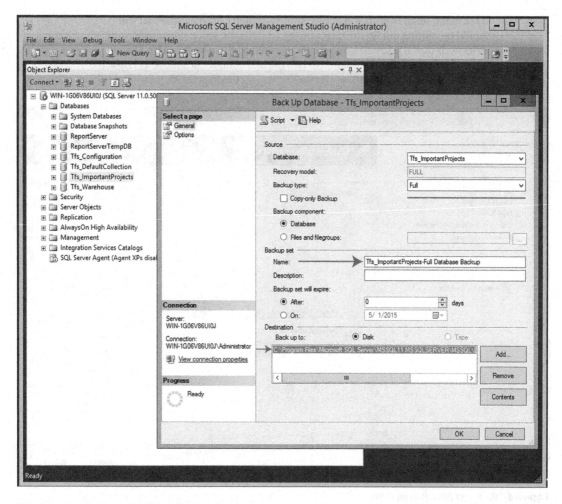

Figure 4-19. *Back up the TFS collection database so you can move it*

11. Once the backup is complete, you need to move it to its new home and attach it. There are many ways to do this, such as using the Copy Database Wizard that you can access from the SQL Server Management Studio. Just right-click the database and select Tasks ➤ Copy Database, and it will take you through the steps. This tool lets you move server to server without having to worry about where to put a file, and so forth. A note of caution here: you can only do this with a version identical or higher than your own. If you need to, you can find more information about the Copy Database Wizard at https://msdn.microsoft.com/en-us/library/ms188664.aspx. At this point, you could put the detached database on a different SQL server or TFS server in your implementation. The reattachment is easy; you'll go through it next.

12. Back to the Team Foundation Server Administration Console. Note that you should be starting this on the target server, which is the server you moved your collections to. If it is just to a different SQL instance, it can be the same TFS server. From the Team Foundation Server Administration Console, select **Attach Collection** (see Figure 4-20).

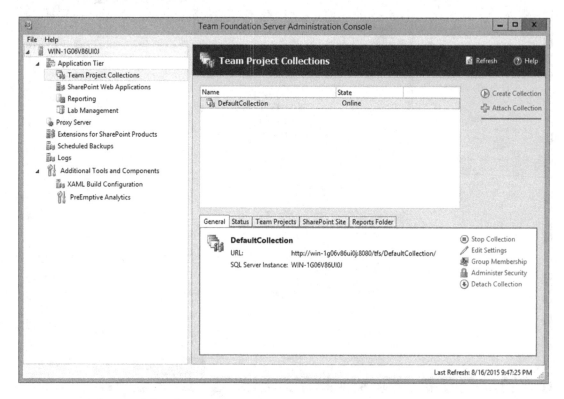

Figure 4-20. *Select Attach from here*

13. When the wizard starts, it automatically finds available but unattached databases on the current SQL Server instance. If you need to select a different one, just type in the instance and hit the **List Available Databases** link to refresh the list (see Figure 4-21). When ready, confirm the backup and schema update warnings. I want to share a few caveats that are important to point out before you continue that will generate warnings during the process. First, if you are on a new server, and your implementation uses SharePoint products, make sure that the Service Account for TFS is in the Farm Administrators group. Second, if you used Reporting, don't try to re-create the exact folder and path that the reports were in on the old server (the process does this for you and generates the default reports). None of these would stop you, but figured I'd mention it. When you are ready, hit **Next**.

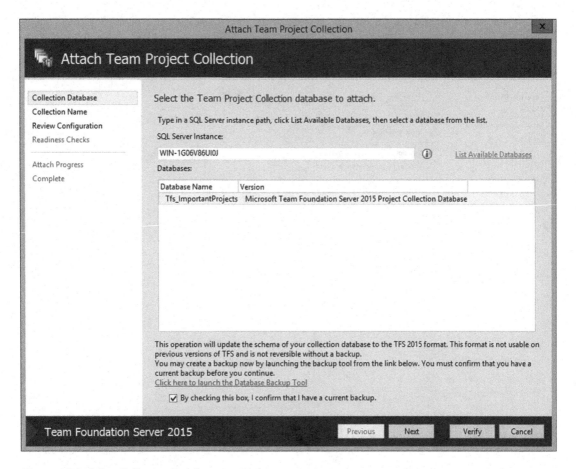

Figure 4-21. *Select Collection Database to attach*

14. Next, you can enter the collection's name and description (see Figure 4-22). Click
Next when ready.

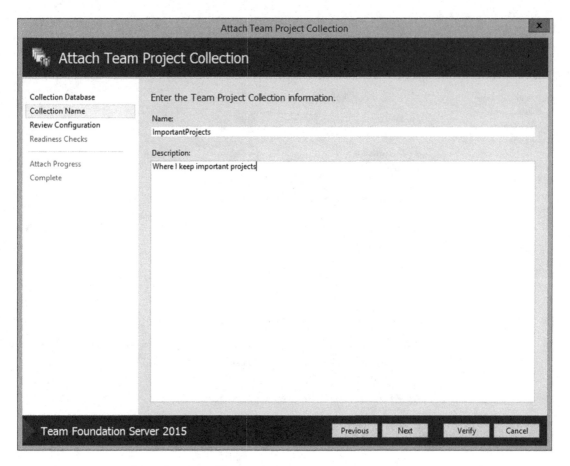

Figure 4-22. *Name and describe your collection*

15. Confirm your settings; they should be similar to what you see in Figure 4-23. Click **Verify** when ready.

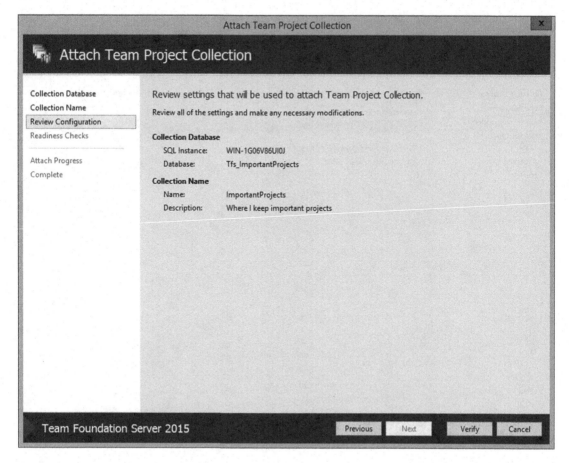

Figure 4-23. *Confirmation*

16. Next, click **Verify** to run the readiness checks. Hopefully, you get the all-clear, as seen in Figure 4-24. When you are ready, click **Attach**.

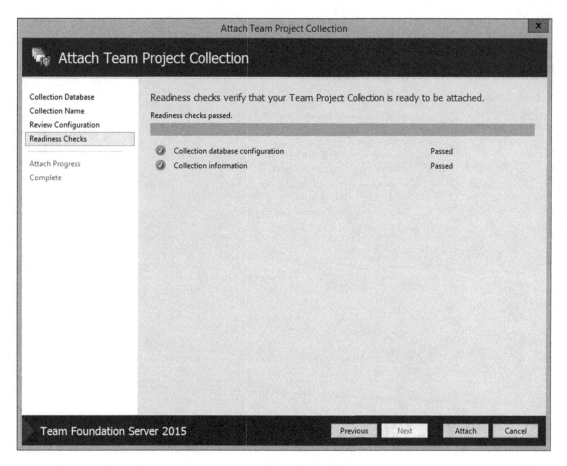

Figure 4-24. *Readiness checks passed*

17. In Figure 4-25 and Figure 4-26, you can see the results of this attach. Earlier I mentioned that a report path and folder already existed; you can see the results. This warning is simply informational in this case, so you can continue.

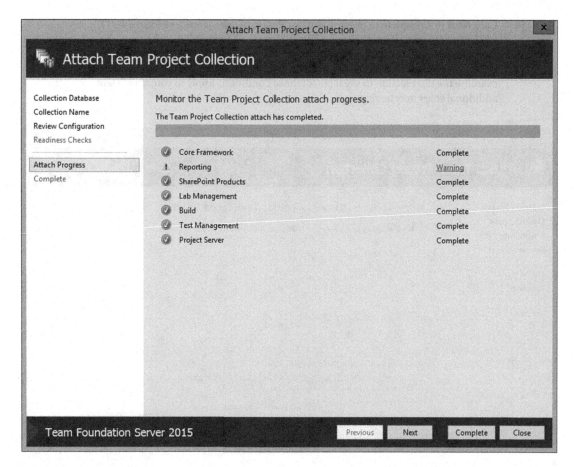

Figure 4-25. *Attach results*

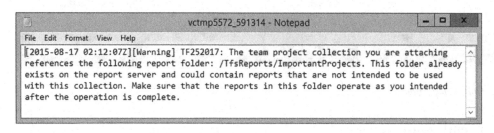

Figure 4-26. *Warning log*

18. Click **Next** or **Complete** to move to the last screen of the wizard (see Figure 4-27), where you are offered another opportunity to review the warning. Since you have already done this, you are all set. Your "moved" collection is now attached; but there are a few final steps to complete. Click **Close** to exit the wizard. Please examine the next section to see if any of those conditions apply to you; if so, a few additional steps may be required.

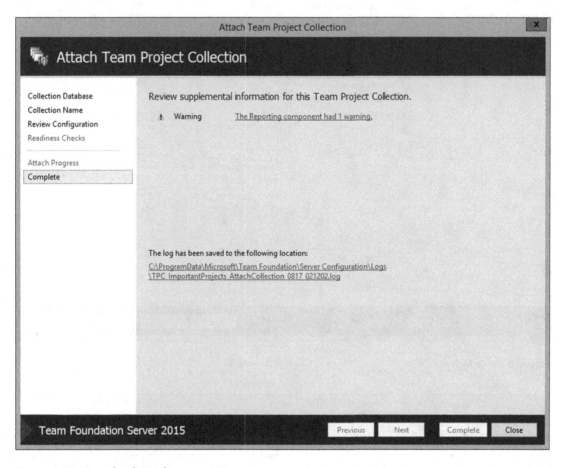

Figure 4-27. *Completed Attach*

Collections with Reports

If you had no customized reports in your collection, then you have nothing more to do with reports. A new default set was installed when you attached the collection. However, if you do have them, you'll likely want to move them over. This is a fairly tedious process, since, believe it or not, you have no wizard for it. And you'll need to do work for each report you bring over, so best to go through your report server and identify the subset of modified reports you want. There are a number of ways to get the reports over the new server as well, but in this case, I'm going to recommend directly publishing them to the new server since this is the most direct way. Finally, you need to rebuild the data warehouse and Analysis Services databases.

1. Once you identified the reports to move, go to the **Report Builder** on the original server. Open the report in Report Builder and select **Save As**.

2. From here, select the new server instance and save it to the new folder location on the new server.

3. Once this is done, you need to open the same report on the new server in Report Builder and reset its data source property to the new server. More information on this process is available at `https://msdn.microsoft.com/en-us/library/dd255213(v=sql.110).aspx`.

4. The last steps are to rebuild the data warehouse and Analysis Services databases on the new server. Go to Team Foundation Server Administration Console ➤ Reporting. Select **Start Rebuild**. Depending on the size of the databases, this could take several hours to finish, so plan accordingly.

Collections with SharePoint

If the collection that you moved uses SharePoint products, you may have a few more steps to do. Primarily, cleaning up the old SharePoint site on the source server, and moving the SharePoint site to the destination server. It's not hard, and you're probably wondering why the wizard couldn't do this for you. Me too, and it's in as a suggestion for a future release. So rather than waiting, here's how you go about getting it done.

First, let's back up the site collection database. This can be an involved process (but doesn't need to be), so I'm only going to cover it at a high level here for SharePoint 2013 (since most of you are using that by now). For more detailed information, please visit `https://technet.microsoft.com/library/ee748617(v=office.15).aspx`. There are a number of ways to back up the site collection; I'm using SharePoint Central Administration here.

1. Navigate to Start ➤ SharePoint 2013 Central Administration. In the Backup and Restore area of the page, click **Perform a Sight Collection Backup**.

2. Next, you'll select the site collection. By default, this tool will just get you the root site collection. Select the **Site Collection** drop-down menu and in the pop-up dialog, choose the site collection that belongs with your TFS collection. Back on the main screen, enter a backup file and path. (Resist the temptation to send this directly to a UNC path, as shown—performance will be horrible!) Here you are working with the sample ImportantProjects collection, as shown in Figure 4-28. When ready, select **Start Backup**. It will look as if nothing is happening for a bit while the backup is occurring, but with any luck, you'll eventually get the success screen shown in Figure 4-29.

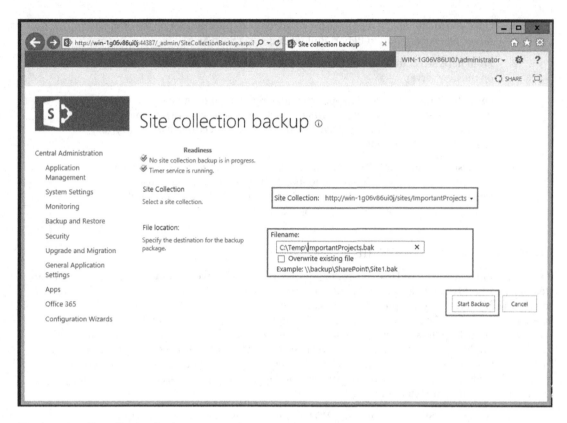

Figure 4-28. Site collection backup

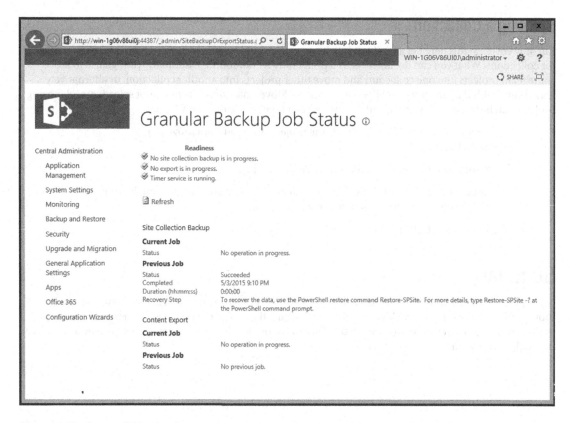

Figure 4-29. Successful backup!

3. Next, use whatever method works for you to copy the backup file to the new server. From this point, open the SharePoint 2013 Central Administration on the receiving server. On the Home screen in the **Backup and Restore** section, select **Restore from a backup** and specify the file. Follow the prompts to complete.

4. Once this is done, you need to link SharePoint with the TFS collection by running a repair on it. Go to the **Team Foundation Administrators Console** on the receiving server and select **SharePoint Web Applications**. From here, select your restored site collection and click **Repair** on the right side of the screen. The wizard will guide you through the rest and you'll have your moved collection back online. An optional last step would be to remove the site collection from the server you moved it from—to keep things neat and tidy. Go to the **SharePoint 2013 Central Administration** application on the original server and select Application Management ➤ Delete a Site Collection. Select the old site collection on the dialog. Click **Delete**.

An optional step is to remove the SharePoint web application from the SharePoint server. To do this, simply go back to the source Team Foundation Server, pen SharePoint Central Administration, and delete the site collection that supports the now moved collection. The same rule would apply to deleting a site collection for a deleted project collection.

Splitting a Collection

I'm only covering this here because if I didn't, its absence would be conspicuous. There is no real "split" for collections. What you can do, however, is a pretty nifty work-around. Essentially, your goal is to move some team projects into one collection and move other projects into another collection, or alternatively, leave them behind in the original collection. Since the Move Collection process is not selective, and moving projects can be tedious, this isn't a bad compromise. It is generally done as follows:

1. Determine which collection holds the projects that you want moved to the new server.

2. Perform a normal move, as described in this chapter.

3. On the new server, simply delete the team projects that you do not want, leaving only the ones that you wanted to move.

Not elegant, but it gets the job done.

Summary

Team project collections were covered in detail in this chapter, starting with usage considerations and moving through creating, managing, moving, and splitting them. The chapter also covered site collection backup and restore after a move (more on this later in the book). Next, you'll look at team projects and learn how to best use them.

CHAPTER 5

■ ■ ■

Managing Team Projects

In the last chapter, you looked at team collections. This chapter examines team projects, a Team Foundation Server structure that acts a place for our source code and allows us to collaborate on software development activities— all in one handy container. This chapter covers

- Team projects overview and usage
- Setting up projects
- Security
- Source control choices

Team Projects Overview

Team projects have been around since TFS's introduction. Team projects form the secondary container in the source code hierarchy (within Visual Studio, there is also Solutions and Projects), work items, tests, workflows, and build information. Team projects contain Visual Studio projects; the hierarchy is depicted in Figure 5-1. If the TFS data tier looks unfamiliar, please flip back to Chapter 4 and take a look at Figure 4-1.

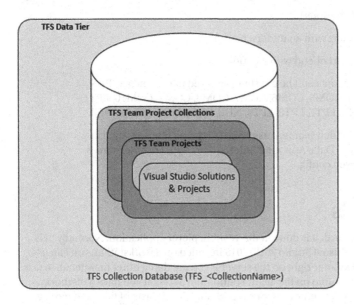

Figure 5-1. *Team project collection to team project relationship*

This often ends up as a point of confusion for developers who have only worked in Visual Studio while not connected to TFS or another source control system.

Team Project Boundaries

Generally, you want your entire software product in a single team project. The reason is manyfold but the key is that is that all the collaboration tools in Team Foundation Server use it as a boundary, making working across the boundry possible but fairly challenging. I haven't seen this as too huge of a problem for people, in general, but there is always a first time, so just be aware of the team's needs when setting up team project. There is no longer a hard limit on the number of team projects in a team project collection until resources on the server become overly constrained. There is specific guidance on this in Chapter 1.

The only time I see that a deliberate separation makes sense is when there are certain segments of your development community using a third-party tool that integrates at the team project level. This can occur if there is multiplatform development involved; however, that multiplatform development on its own is not a reason to break that segment off on its own.

Team Project Naming Conventions

The naming conventions for projects will look familiar; they are the same as collections. You cannot use spaces or reserved characters when you create one (more later in this chapter). The following are a number of naming convention restrictions that you'll want to keep in mind:

- *Length*: No more than 64 Unicode characters

- *Uniqueness*: A project name can't be identical to any other project name in your team project collection. Here are the rules on special characters:

  - No Unicode control characters or surrogate characters

  - None of these printable characters: / : \ ~ & % ; @ ' " ? < > | # $ * } { , + = [ ]

  - No ellipsis (...) or double periods (..)

  - The project name can't start with an underscore (_)

  - The project name can't start or end with a period (.)

- *Reserved names*: The project name can't be a system-reserved name, such as PRN, COM1, COM2, COM3, COM4, COM5, COM6, COM7, COM8, COM9, COM10, LPT1, LPT2, LPT3, LPT4, LPT5, LPT6, LPT7, LPT8, LPT9, NUL, CON, AUX, Web, or WEB

- The project name can't be a hidden segment used for IIS request filtering, such as App_Browsers, App_code, App_Data, App_GlobalResources, App_LocalResources, App_WebResources, bin, or web.config.

Setting up Team Projects

Creating team projects is fairly straightforward; it is done in the Team Explorer application. Normally, it is installed with Visual Studio, so if you have Visual Studio 2013/2015 installed on a workstation, you can use that. Alternatively, you can install Team Explorer right on the server if you are doing other maintenance tasks on the server. You could also install Visual Studio on the Team Foundation Server if you have a plethora of licenses; but unless you are just doing lab experiments, this is probably just a waste of time and money. Team Explorer is only available as a separate application with Visual Studio 2013 and prior.

Where team project collections were set up with the TFS Administrations Console, team projects need to be created from a Visual Studio client (it can be the free Visual Studio Community Edition). In the following examples, you are using Visual Studio 2015. If you are using an account that is different from the one that you installed TFS with, you need to add it to the project collection Administrators group before you begin. If you successfully walked through the collection creation process in the last chapter, you should be all set; however, there are a few other processes that you need to undertake to successfully create projects. Let's cover these first.

Reporting Services Permissions to View or Create Reports

If you are using the same account you used while installing TFS, you are probably all set. However, if you are just now picking up this book, let's take a look. You need to be a member of the Team Foundation Content Manager group.

1. To do this, go to the **Report Manager** home page in Internet Explorer; typically, it is at an address such as `http://<report server name>:80/Reports`. If you can't find yours, open the Team Foundation Server Administration Console and go to the **Application Tier ➤ Reporting** node to look it up. Once on the Reports home page, select **Folder Settings**, as indicated in Figure 5-2.

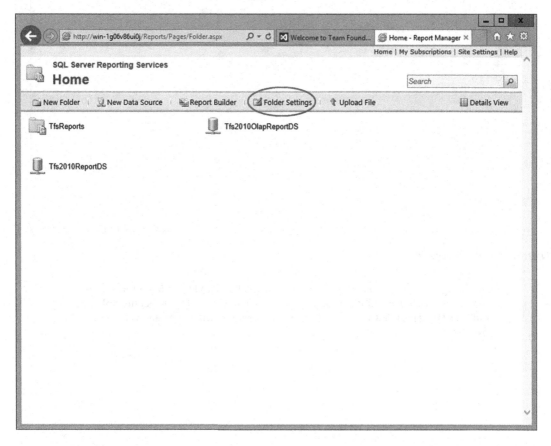

Figure 5-2. *Reports home page*

2. This brings you to the Security screen. You can see in Figure 5-3 that both the Administrator account and our TFSSERVICE account were already added to the Team Foundation Content Manager group. You are going to add another user account to that role as an example. Select **New Role Assignment**, as indicated in Figure 5-3.

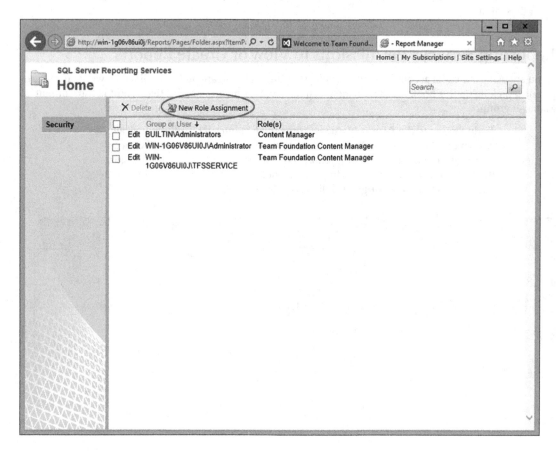

Figure 5-3. *Reports Security*

3. This brings you to the Role Assignment screen, as shown in Figure 5-4. From here, you enter the account or group you want the Role added to. Select the **Role** and click **OK**. This takes you back to the Settings screen, where you can verify the results.

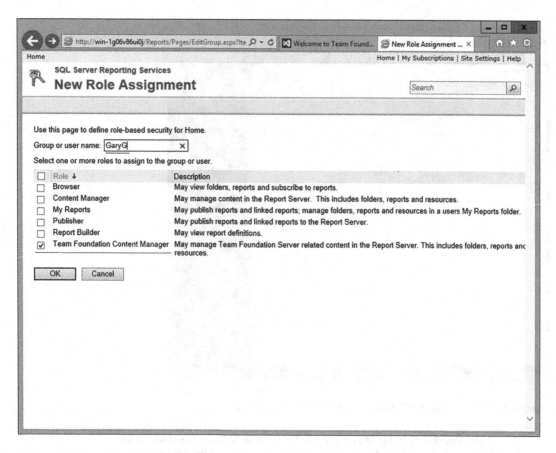

Figure 5-4. *New Role Assignment entry screen*

SQL Server Database Roles for Report Authors and to Create Team Projects

Now that the Reporting Services is all set, you need to add the account to the TfsWarehouseDataReader role for the account you'll use to create the Team project. You also need to do this for any user that needs to create customized reports in Reporting Services. It is very straightforward, but you will be using a different tool: Microsoft SQL Server Management Studio.

1. Go to **Start ➤ Microsoft SQL Server 2012 ➤ Microsoft SQL Server Management Studio**. From here, select **Database Engine** (likely the default), which is your TFS SQL instance (this may not be the default) and click **Connect**, as shown in Figure 5-5.

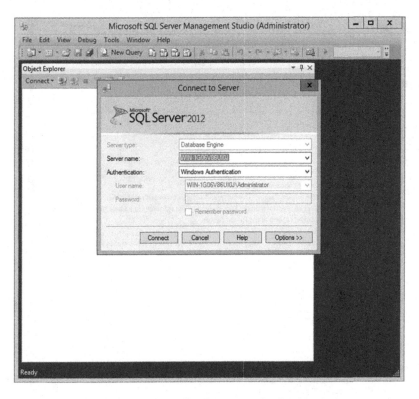

Figure 5-5. *SQL Management Studio: Connect to database engine*

2. Select **Databases ➤ Tfs_Warehouse ➤ Security ➤ Roles ➤ Database Roles**.
   Right-click the **TfsWarehouseDataReader** role and select **Properties**. This pops
   up the **Database Roles Properties** dialog for this role. You can see the Role
   Members in this dialog in the lower pane. Select **Add**, as shown in Figure 5-6.
   Note that the role owner is Dbo (tied to the Windows Administrator account), so
   you are all set. For an example, I'm adding the GaryG account.

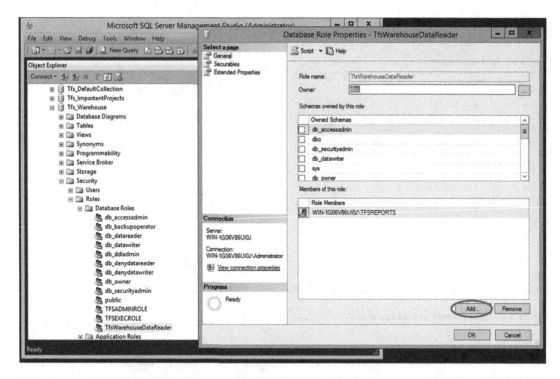

Figure 5-6. *Database Role Properties: TfsDataWarehouseDataReader*

■ **Note**   It's probably important to note that any user you give this role to can view data across all projects. This cannot be restricted to a particular collection or team project at this time.

---

3. As shown in the dialog in Figure 5-7, enter the account and click **OK**. This returns you to the previous window to verify that it was successfully added as a member of the role (see Figure 5-8). Click **OK**.

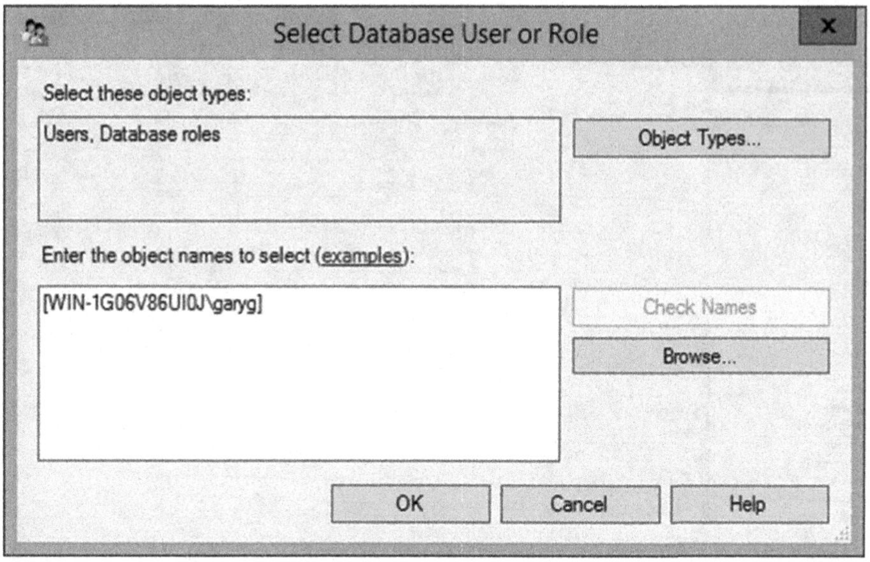

Figure 5-7. *Select a user to add to the role*

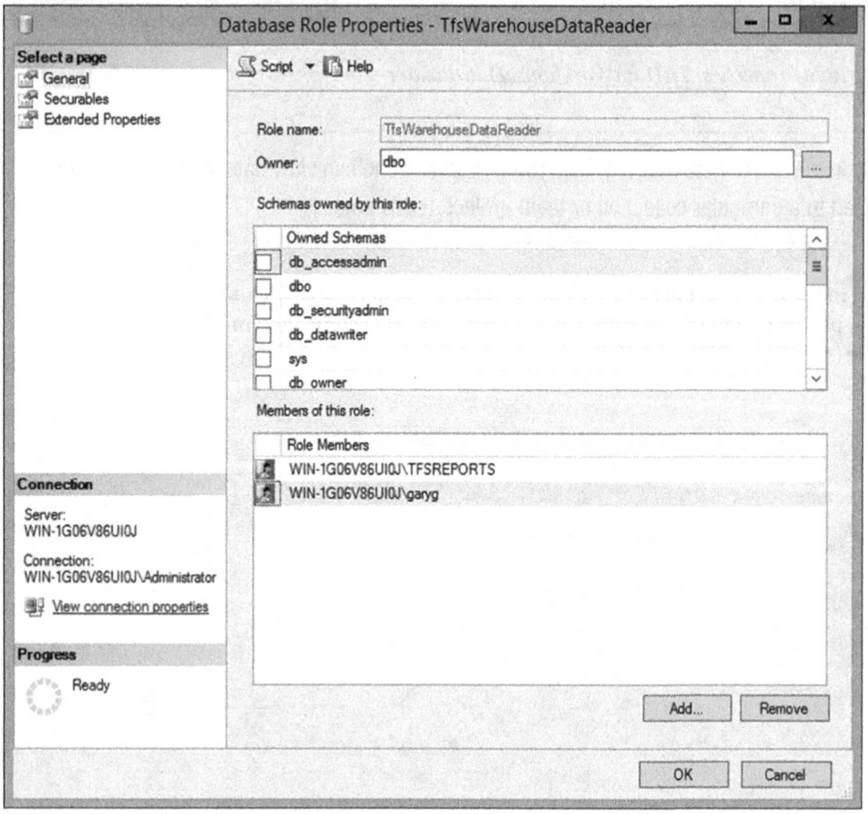

Figure 5-8. *User added*

Check to Make Sure That You Are in the Project Collection Administrators Group

Again, you are probably all set if you are still using the account you installed TFS with, but I want to point out how to get here if you are in an enterprise environment or if you just want to use a different account. As with many aspects of TFS, there are multiple ways to do things. You can perform collection-level security maintenance from either the Team Foundation Administration Console (a tool you've used frequently throughout the book) or you can use Team Web Access. For variety's sake, I'll demonstrate with Team Web Access.

1. Let's set up an account. Open Internet Explorer and go to your Team Web Access address. Typically, it is at `http://<tfsservername>:8080/tfs`. Then click the **Administer** panel, as shown in Figure 5-9. This opens the Team Web Access Control Panel, as shown in Figure 5-10.

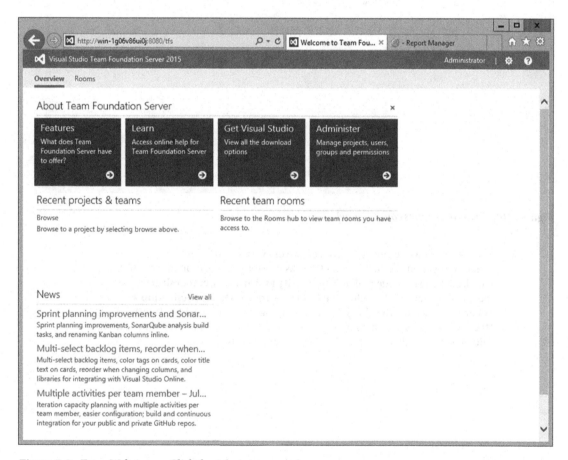

Figure 5-9. *Team Web Access: Click the Administer panel*

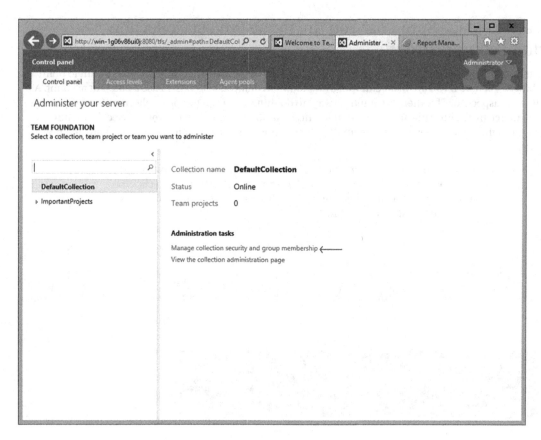

Figure 5-10. *Team Web Access control panel*

2. You are prompted to select the collection you want to work with. DefaultCollection is selected, which works fine for us here. From the control panel, click the **Manage collection security and group membership** link, as indicated in Figure 5-10. Select the **Control Panel ➤ DefaultCollection ➤ Security**. Select the **Members** link in the top right and then **Add ➤ Windows User or Group**, as indicated in Figure 5-11. Fill in the information required in the **Add** dialog, as shown in Figure 5-12. Click **Save Changes**.

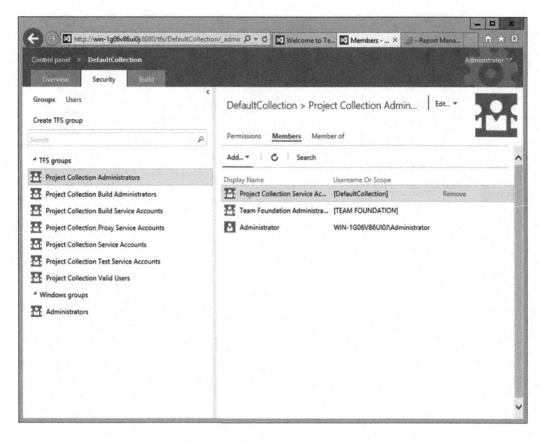

Figure 5-11. *Manage group membership: add a user to a group*

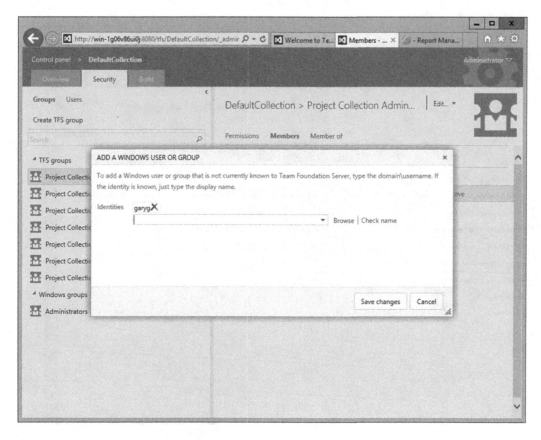

Figure 5-12. *Add Windows User or Group dialog*

SharePoint Permissions

This is another process in which you are likely all set if you are still using the account that you used to install TFS, but if you switched or want enable another account to create team projects, you need to make sure that they are part of the Farm Administrators group in SharePoint.

1. This is very easy. Go to **Start ➤ SharePoint 2013 Products ➤ SharePoint Central Administration** and select the **Manage the farm administrators group**, as indicated in Figure 5-13.

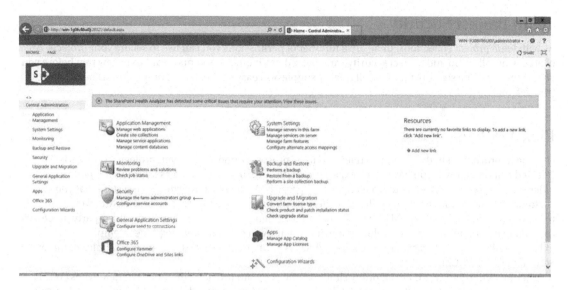

Figure 5-13. *SharePoint Central Administration*

2. This brings you to the **People and Groups ➤ Farm Administrators** screen, where you can add a new account to enable the creation of team projects. Select **New ➤ Add Users to this group** and in the pop-up dialog, add the account you want to enable, as shown in Figure 5-14. I'd recommend using the machine name\username or domain\username format, as I did here, if there are a lot of users. Click **Share** when you are ready. That's it.

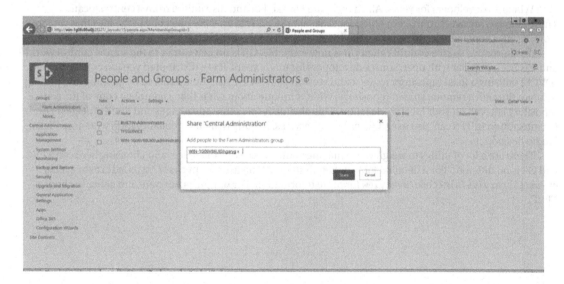

Figure 5-14. *People and Groups: Farm Administrators*

Team Project Security

As with team project collections, there are a number of permissions you can use to secure your projects. An overview of collection and project security was covered in Chapter 3. You may want to review that before you go further here. The security model itself is fairly simple and easy to use. It uses only Allow, Deny, Not Set (the default).

Pick a Process

One big improvement in the latest TFS release is in its process support. In a team project, a process is selected at its creation. If you have some experience with TFS, this was known as a *process template* in older releases; now it just refers to what creates the process. A process is an extensible system that you can customize to match your existing application lifecycle management process. It is fairly easy to work with processes, which are based in XML (extensible markup language). There are also some third-party processes that you may want to search and explore. More information on customizing the process templates is at `https://msdn.microsoft.com/en-us/library/ms243782.aspx`. Out of the box, you get a choice of three: Scrum, Agile, and CCMI.

Scrum, Agile, and CCMI are all pretty similar at the core, but provide different work item types (WIT) to help with planning and tracking work. Of the three, Scrum is considered the most lightweight, whereas CMMI provides some change control and other formalized development processes. For complete details on each one, surf on over to `https://msdn.microsoft.com/library/vs/alm/work/guidance/choose-process`. For our purposes, I'm going to choose Scrum, which is what I use most of the time.

Source Control Choices

Now (well, actually for a few releases now) you have a choice in source control. You can stick with Team Foundation Version Control (TFVC), which is the classic centralized version control that has been popular with Windows developers for years. All changes are checked in and distributed from a central location. These changes are synchronized in either local or server workspaces. Only one copy of the files that you are working on is kept in these workspaces; the history is kept on the server.

An alternative source control called Git is now available. Git is no newcomer to the source control world and has been popular with open source developers for many years. It is a distributed version control system (DVCS) utilizing a local repository to track and version your files. Changes are shared by pushing and pulling changes through a remote, shared repository. What is unique about Git is that a complete copy of the source repository is saved on your local workstation. This obviously has some advantages and disadvantages. The Git integration in TFS can also use third-party Git services, making it ideal for collaboration with non–Visual Studio developers.

There are a lot of things to weigh when making your source control choice, and choosing between TFVC and Git is no different. For a detailed look at their differences, please visit `https://msdn.microsoft.com/en-us/Library/vs/alm/code/overview` for more information. For our purposes here, I'm going to choose TFVC.

Setting up a Team Project

Now for the fun part. You are going to add a team project to the DefaultCollection. You'll use Visual Studio 2015.

1. Open Visual Studio 2015. In the Team Explorer applet, as seen in Figure 5-15 (you can display it from the View menu if it's not on the screen yet), click **Manage Connections** to bring up the **Connect to Team Foundation Server** dialog, as shown in Figure 5-16. Note that the server name is normally populated in the dialog if you are running on the server locally, as I was here; if you are not, just click the Server button to enter one. In the **Team Project Collections** pane, you can pick any *one* that is available. When ready, click **Connect**.

Figure 5-15. *Team Explorer in Visual Studio 2015*

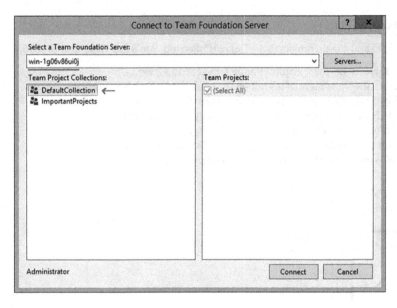

Figure 5-16. *Connect to TFS Server dialog*

2. Next, click the **Home** drop-down list and select **Projects and My Teams ➤ New Team Project...**, as shown in Figure 5-17.

Figure 5-17. *Team Explorer: New Team Project*

3. In the dialog, enter a name and (optionally) a description for your team project, as shown in Figure 5-18. Click **Next** when ready.

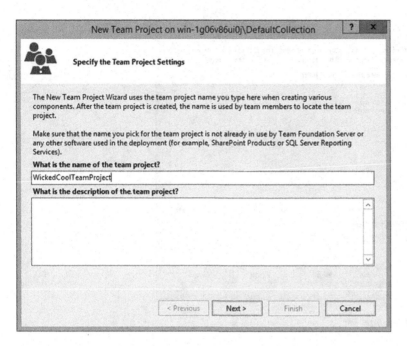

Figure 5-18. *New Team Project: name and description*

4. In the next dialog, select a process template for your project. Making the right selection is important, because switching afterward is a difficult process. These templates select the format and type of work items that you will be using in the project (artifact to track work). Please see the "Pick a Process" section in this chapter for more information. I'm going to choose **Scrum** (see Figure 5-19). Click **Next** when ready.

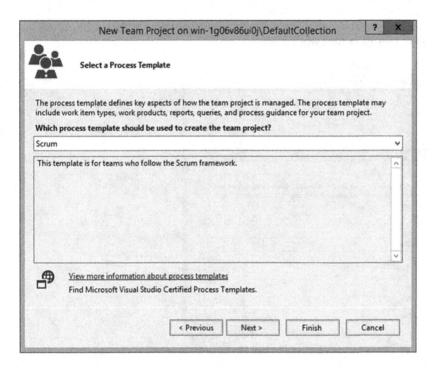

Figure 5-19. *Select a Process Template*

5. In the next section, you get to configure a SharePoint site for our team project. The wizard automatically suggests a site name at the SharePoint server on your TFS configuration, but the Configure button (see Figure 5-20) allows you to change the site name if you need to. Click **Next** when ready.

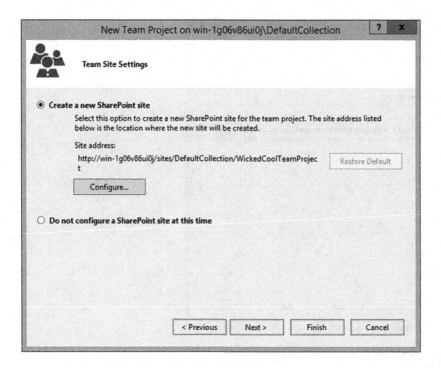

Figure 5-20. SharePoint Site for our team project

6. Next, you pick the source control. You have a choice of two, as presented in in Figure 5-21. TFVC (Team Foundation Version Control) is what I selected here. Please see the "Source Control Choices" section for more information on this. Click **Next** when ready.

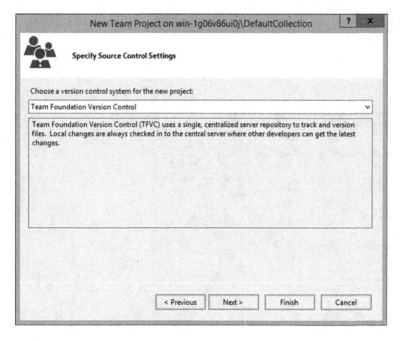

Figure 5-21. Source Control Selection

7. Next is the summary screen. Please review your selections, as shown in Figure 5-22, and click Finish.

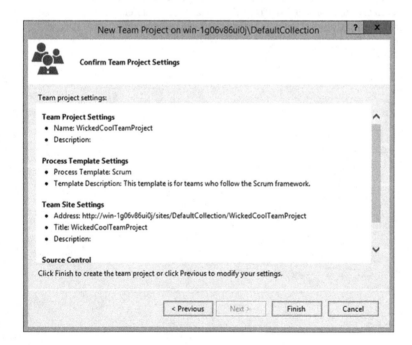

Figure 5-22. Summary

8.   Finally, you come to the progress screen, as shown in Figure 5-23. It updates you on the progress of your team project creation. As the dialog indicates, this process could take a bit of time; typically, I see it take 2 to 10 minutes, depending on the server configuration. If all goes well, you'll next see the confirmation screen, which should look like Figure 5-24. In this dialog, you have the option of displaying the process guidance for the process you chose and a link to the creation log. Click **Close**. You see the process guidance in a web browser. Also, you are now able to see your new team project in the Visual Studio Source Control Explorer, as shown in Figure 5-25.

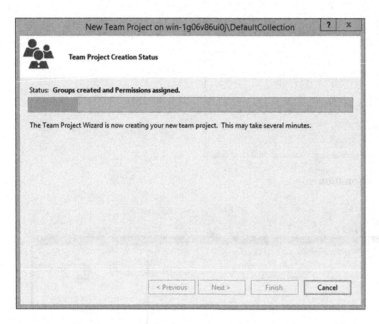

Figure 5-23. *Team project creation progress*

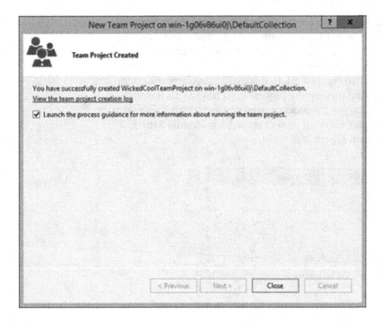

Figure 5-24. *Team project created confirmation*

Figure 5-25. *Your new team project*

Summary

This chapter covered team project boundaries, naming conventions, considerations for creating team projects, and a complete walkthrough of the creation of a team project. The usage of team projects is covered in upcoming chapters.

CHAPTER 6

■ ■ ■

Managing Source Code and Work

Now that you learned how to create team projects, you can begin using them to manage and coordinate development work. In this chapter, you'll look at

- Storing and managing source code

- Branching and merging

- Managing work with agile tools

We aren't going to cover all of Visual Studio's features in this chapter. That would take a few volumes of its own. There are some very advanced features included at all license levels that I'd encourage everyone to check out. What I'll cover here are the key aspects of using Visual Studio with Team Foundation Server. You may also want to jump over to Team Web Access on occasion for certain tasks, so you'll hit some spots where that makes sense as well.

Working with Source Code: Workspaces

In order to begin working with source code, you need to either configure a workspace (those who use TFVC) or clone the repository (if you are using Git). Since we used TFVC, you'll need to set up your workspace. You have a choice here of using local or server workspaces.

Server or Local?

Server workspaces are the classical method of working with source code. Prior to TFS 2012, they were called just "workspaces." There were always local portions, but there were several key data structures that needed a constant connection to the server, which occurred when

- Opening a source-controlled solution

- Checking out a file for edit

- Pending a new file or folder to add

- Pending a delete on an existing file or folder

- Pending a rename on an existing file or folder

- Asking "what are the pending changes in this workspace?"

- Undoing pending changes

- Diffing your copy of a file with the version of the file your change is pended against

All of this can now be done while disconnected with a local workspace. Of course, there are a number of items that still require an active connection, like using the Source Control Explorer (this one kills me, use it all the time), viewing the history of an item, checking in, shelving/unshelving, branching/merging, undeleting items, and just about every item dealing with managing source. So why do local workspace make sense? You'll consider that by just planning ahead a little now you can take what you need for offline use like in a plane or off the network somewhere. There are a couple of other things with local workspaces to keep in mind too:

- *No longer just read-only*. In server workspaces, everything but the items you checked out is marked read-only. Not so in local workspaces. When pending changes are scanned by Visual Studio, you don't go back to the server to look for checked out files; the checkout is implicit. These can be seen in Team Explorer in the Pending Changes.

- *Change candidate*. The TFVC workspace scanner looks for any changes, adds, deletes, and creates a *change candidate*. The Team Explorer has a link to examine the changes and pops up the Promote Candidate Changes dialog, where you can look at the changes. You'll check this out later.

- *Pend Change Permission*. Due to the features in the local workspace, this can no longer be enforced. Check-in locks seem to work, but taking or releasing a check-in lock requires a server connection.

- *Conversion*. You can convert back and forth from either type of workspace. The Edit Workspace dialog is where you manage this (You need to have the Advanced button to see this option). I'll go over doing this later in the chapter.

- *Performance*. What is the impact, either way, on performance and scalability? It's best to limit local workspaces to small or medium-sized projects. Not only are you looking at an about a 50% increase in local disk space, but if you have more than 50,000 files, you may end up getting an error. Server workspaces can scale up to 10 million files by contrast. If you still want to work with larger projects in local workspaces, I'd suggest splitting them up into smaller workspaces by only taking certain branches into each one.

Setting up the Workspace

Now you'll get a workspace set up for use. For our examples here, you'll use a server workspace since it has the most universal application. Let's step through it.

1. In Team Explorer in Visual Studio, follow the links to **Project ➤ Configure Workspace**, as shown in Figure 6-1.

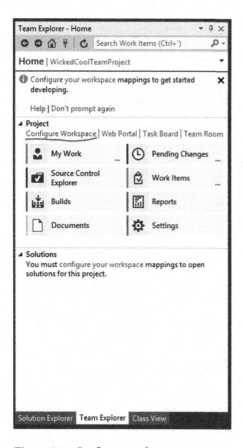

Figure 6-1. *Configure workspace*

2.   In the next window (see Figure 6-2), you see the Configure Workspace pane. Here you can accept the defaults (grabs the current place in the team project) and the default source location which is <user profile>\Source\Workspaces\<Workspace Name>. These look good for now, so you'll take these and click the **Map & Get** button as indicated. Alternatively, you could have clicked the **Advanced** link and performed more extensive workspace configuration, including additional mappings and location.

Figure 6-2. *Configure Workspace panel*

3. After you map and get the workspace, you should see a notification that it was successful, as shown in Figure 6-3. You also see that the local path is now defined in the Source Control Explorer header, as shown in Figure 6-4.

Figure 6-3. *Success notice*

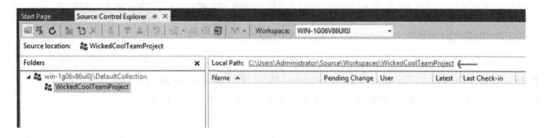

Figure 6-4. *Local path defined*

Adding a Solution/Project to a Team Project

Next, you need to add a Visual Studio solution or project to our TFS team project. Microsoft made this process fairly simple. It can be done as you create new solutions or projects by selecting the **Add to source control** check box in the Visual Studio New Project dialog, as shown in Figure 6-5, or by adding it from an existing local one.

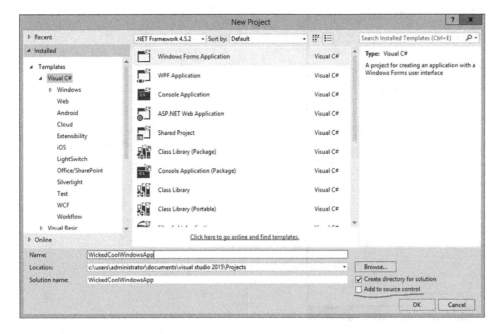

Figure 6-5. *Add to Source check box*

Although adding a new solution while creating it is fairly self-explanatory, getting an existing one may not be. While in Visual Studio (this is assuming the solution/project is in Visual Studio; if not, please consult that documentation), navigate to Solution Explorer (the tab next to Team Explorer).

■ **Note** If Team Explorer or Solution Explorer become hidden or closes accidently, you can always get them back by going to **View ➤ Team Explorer or View ➤ Solution Explorer** in Visual Studio.

---

1. Once in Solution Explorer, just right-click a solution and select **Add to Solution to Source Control** from the menu, as shown in Figure 6-6.

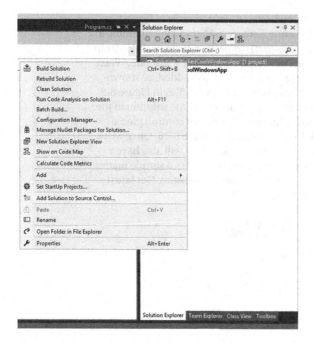

Figure 6-6. *Add Solution to Source Control*

2. In the dialog shown in Figure 6-7, you can see that you need to tell Visual Studio if you are going to be working with TFS. Please select **Team Foundation Version Control** (I'll discuss Git later in the chapter).

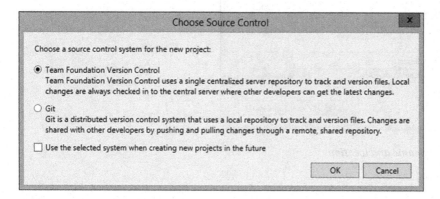

Figure 6-7. *Choose source control*

■ **Note**   If you accidently pick Git as a source control system, you need to close out of Visual Studio and remove the hidden `.git` folder to break that connection. The Remove function in the Team Explorer was not functional for Git as of this writing.

---

3. Next, you pick a location to put the solution in the team project, as indicated in Figure 6-8. You can add a new folder structure here (handy, if you are planning a large app and want to separate various parts of it). By default, it creates a folder in TFS with the same name as the solution. For our purposes, that is just fine. When this is complete, you can see that the project has indeed been added, as shown in Figure 6-9. Please note the little + (plus signs) next to all the files in Figure 6-9 as well. This indicates you have a pending change (our adding the solution to the source). To complete the check-in of the solution to the source control, please go to Team Explorer and select **Check In**, as indicated in Figure 6-10. Once that's complete, you get a confirmation in Team Explorer. The little + will also have disappeared from Source Control Explorer. From here on out, it's a simple matter of right-clicking the project in Source Control Explorer and selecting **Get latest version for updates** (there are other methods as well).

Figure 6-8. Confirm folder name and location

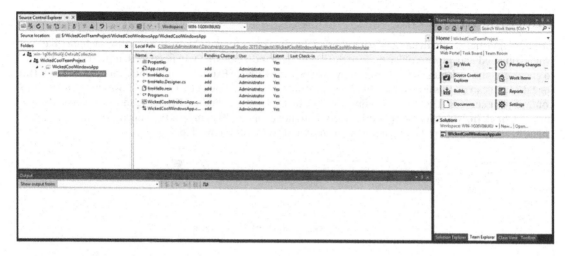

Figure 6-9. *Our solution in Source Control Explorer*

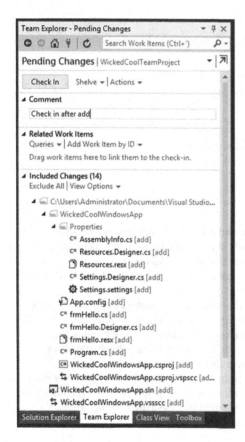

Figure 6-10. *Need to check in our pending changes*

Checking In and Out

Ordinarily, Visual Studio dynamically handles all the checkouts for you. There are situations where (like when you need to beat your office mate to the highly demanded file that you need in 10 minutes) you want to check out and lock files. To do this, simply go to Source Control Explorer. Right-click and select **Check Out for Edit** (you can do this for a bunch of files or an entire solution). You get the dialog shown in Figure 6-11 to confirm your choices. Also, you can adjust the lock type from the default in **Unchanged - Keep any existing lock** or **Check In**, which lets someone check out but not check in. This means they need to do a merge to check in afterward. I'm not doing either at the moment since I don't need to.

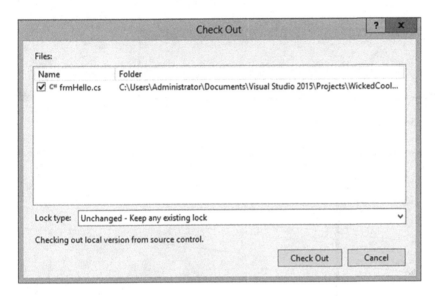

Figure 6-11. *Confirm check out*

Branching and Merging

You could fill up a book only discussing branching and merging and all of their strategies and nuances. I'll cover the highlights here. Branching and merging are methods of reducing risk and increasing stability into your code and process. Imagine that one of your teams wants to engage in an experiment of sorts that requires major components to be replaced. For this, you would create a branch. Do your risky coding in there, prove or disprove the effort, and then merge back to the original if it warrants it.

There are other production or DevOps-oriented scenarios that a branching strategy supports, such as release branches to stabilize releases while continuing the development of a product. Another common strategy allows multiple teams to work concurrently on common features by using feature branches to segregate the code. This is not without complication, as merging these types of changes back into a single branch can create many conflicts that need to be resolved to integrate these changes.

I've only given you a brief overview of what's possible with branching and merging strategies. For more information (if your needs are complex or you are planning an enterprise deployment) I highly recommend reviewing the ALM Ranger Branching and Merging Guide available at http://vsarbranchingguide. codeplex.com/. This guide has gone through several releases and it gets better each time.

Branching

Here, I'll just cover the essentials of creating a branch. In Figure 6-12, you can see that I renamed a few folders and added a Main folder with the intention of putting other solutions there.

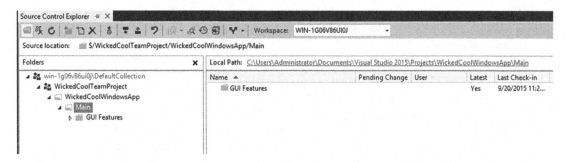

Figure 6-12. *Directories in my team project*

I'm also working with a test team that wants to do some extensive regression testing for me, but I don't want to hold up development while the daylong suite runs. The solution is to create a stable Test branch for the testers to work from.

1. In the Source Control Explorer, you are going to select the **Main** directory. (If it isn't your directory structure, just take a minute to create a Main directory and a GUI Features directory, and then move your solution under them). Select the **Branch** button, as indicated in Figure 6-13, or right-click and select **Branching and Merging ➤ Branch**. This brings up the dialog shown in Figure 6-13; not the target end point, which is the branch. The default is always <the source> - branch. You can change this easily enough, which was done to Test in Figure 6-14. You are also taking the default check boxes to download the target and immediately convert the folder, so that it shows up. Hit **OK** when ready to create the Test branch. After you do this, you need to go to **Team Explorer ➤ Pending Changes** and press **Check In**.

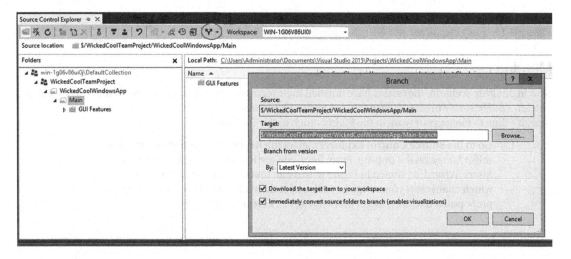

Figure 6-13. *Branch dialog*

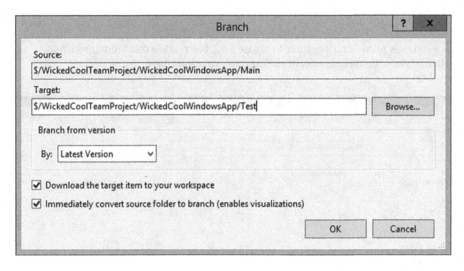

Figure 6-14. Naming the branch test

2. In Figure 6-15, you can see the branch fully visualized. Next, I'll go over merging changes.

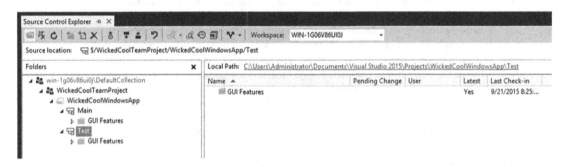

Figure 6-15. Fully visualized Test branch

Merging

Now in our little scenario, the testers have finished their regression testing cycle, thankful that you gave them a steady codebase to work from. Now they are requesting to test what you have been working on all of this time. It's time to merge your work in the Main branch to the Test branch.

1. Go to the **Source Control Explorer**. Select the **Branch Merge** button and then select Merge on the pop-up. From here, you are looking at the Source Control Merge Wizard, as shown in Figure 6-16. Note that you can get selective on which changesets you merge in. Let's select them all here. Also, the wizard was prepopulated with its target branch test. Click **Next** when ready.

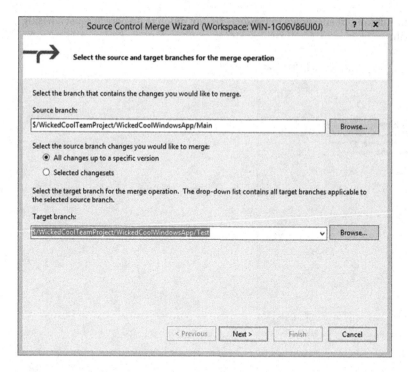

Figure 6-16. *Source Control Merge Wizard*

2. In the next wizard screen, you can choose to merge the latest version, changeset, date, or label. Let's take the default here, as shown in Figure 6-17, and keep going. Click **Next** when ready.

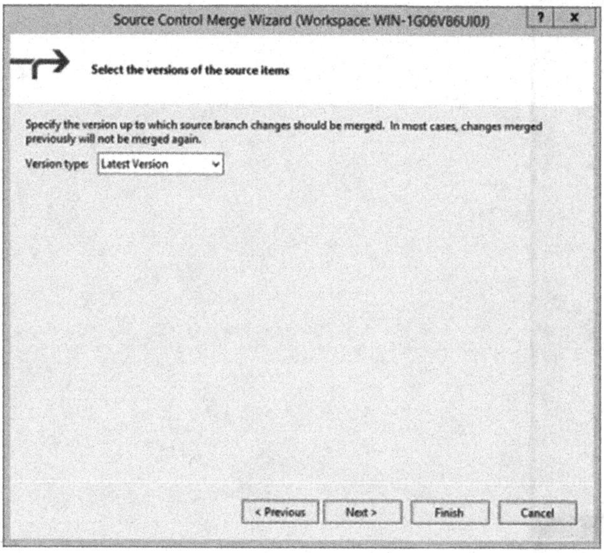

Figure 6-17. *Merge options*

Next, you come to the confirmation screen, shown in Figure 6-18. Not much to do here; it's just advising if you have conflicts. Click **Finish**.

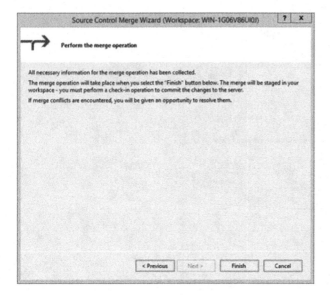

Figure 6-18. *Confirmation*

3. When you click Finish, the wizard closes. If you look over to the Team Explorer panel under pending changes, you'll notice you have a change to commit (I only made one in this case). Click **Check In**, as shown in Figure 6-19, and the merge is done.

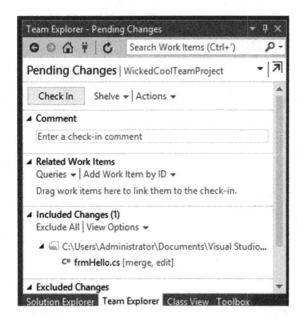

Figure 6-19. *Check in changes after the merge*

Managing Work

If you are working with three or more people these days, you are likely working in an agile framework. You're not? Well, you really should think about it, because most of the industry has switched over to one form or another of agile. If you are unfamiliar with Agile or Scrum (the most prevalent of the agile frameworks), I would suggest a visit to http://www.Scrum.org as a first stop. It was founded by Ken Schwaber, one of the original creators of the Scrum framework.

Luckily, Team Foundation Server has a full set of agile tools to help us collaborate and work together more effectively. I'll go over the basics here You'll create a team (you can have as many as you see fit), get a backlog together, and work with sprints.

Setting up a Team

Agile is all about the team. The first thing you should do is set up a team to work on the project. Before getting started here, I created a few user accounts to work with; you may want to do this, or use actual user accounts if you are ready. You've spent a great deal of time in this chapter in Visual Studio since it is the primary TFS interface for most developers. You are going to jump into the Team Web Access portal for the rest of this of this chapter.

1. To get started, click the gear icon on the Team Web Access portal, as shown in Figure 6-20.

Figure 6-20. *Team Web Access: Select administration*

2. From here, you go to the administration screen. Select your project, as shown in Figure 6-21, and select the link for the **Project Administration Page**, as indicated in Figure 6-22.

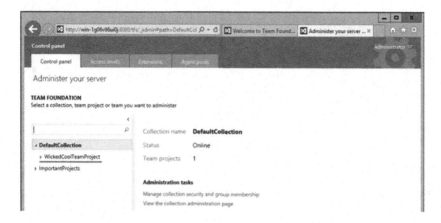

Figure 6-21. *Select your project*

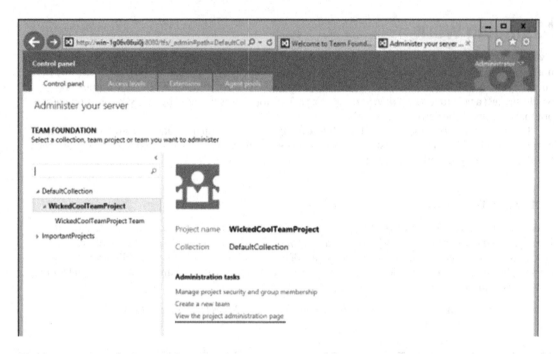

Figure 6-22. *Go to the project administration screen*

3. From the project administration screen, you can see there is already a default team, which was automatically created. You are going to create a new team, so click the **New Team** button, as indicated in Figure 6-23.

Figure 6-23. *Project screen*

4. In the New Team dialog (see Figure 6-24), name the team. Please make sure you have the box selected to create an area path for the team (the area path is a hierarchal categorization used to organize work). You also get to select a security group to add the team to. **Contributors** is the default and works fine in this case. Hit the **Create Team** button when ready.

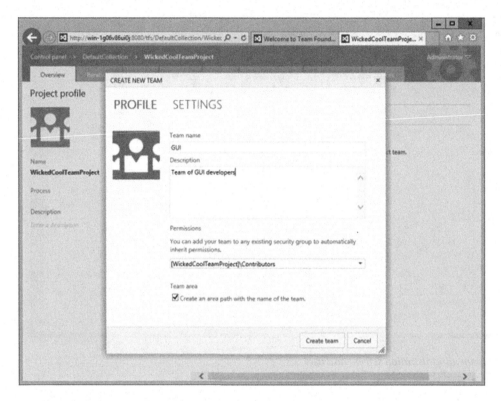

Figure 6-24. *Create team dialog*

5. Click the team name to come to the team administration dialog, as shown in Figure 6-25. From there, click the **Add ➤ Add Windows user or group** button and add in the sample users, as shown in Figure 6-26. Click **Save Changes** when ready, which takes you back to the overview screen so that you can delete and add users.

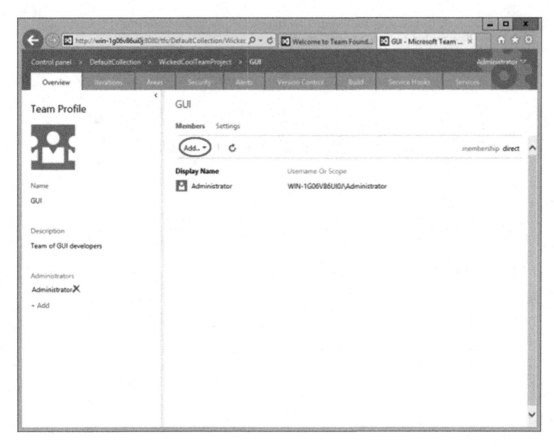

Figure 6-25. *Team administration screen: add user*

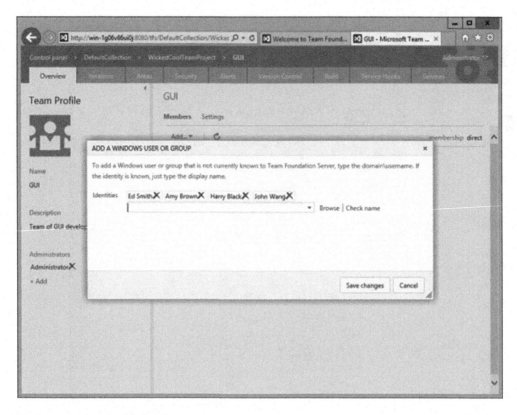

Figure 6-26. *Users added to the team*

6. Now that you have users on the GUI team, you need to set up iterations and sprints for the team to work in. You are back on the Overview page. Click the **Settings** link, as indicated in Figure 6-27. From there, you can pick the types of work items (these are objects in TFS used to track work and defects). On the settings page, as pictured in Figure 6-28, you can select which items you want on your backlog, the working days, and how bugs should appear (for more information on bug appearance options go to https://msdn.microsoft.com/ Library/vs/alm/work/customize/show-bugs-on-backlog). I selected Epics, left the working to the weekday default, and chose to have bugs appear with my bugs on the backlog.

Figure 6-27. Team administration: pick settings

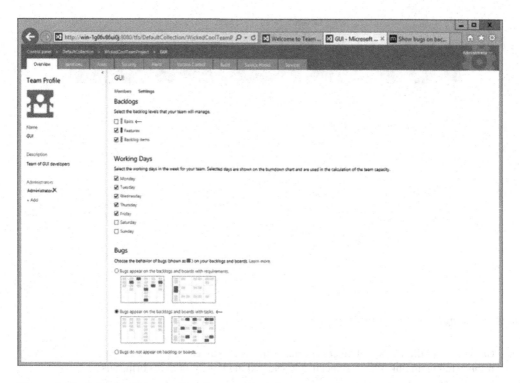

Figure 6-28. *Select backlog, working days, and how bugs appear*

7. Next, click the **Iterations** tab and select the iterations you'll need to work on (see Figure 6-29). Set the first one as the backlog sprint. You can also set the sprint dates. You could set a series of iterations and sprints as children, but for now, I'll just keep it simple. There are a bunch of other options you could look at, like setting more areas to further categorize work, setting security for a team member, build settings, and so forth, but for now, you have enough to continue.

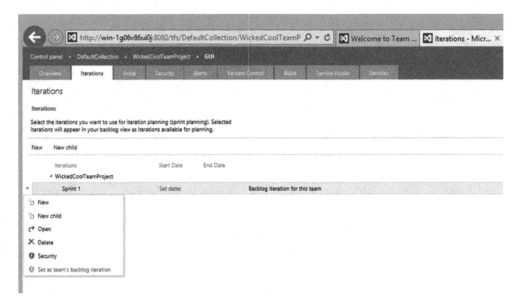

Figure 6-29. *Selecting iterations/sprints and options*

8. Going back to the Team Web Access portal home page, you can see there is a new project and team link. Please select it, as indicated in Figure 6-30. This brings us

Figure 6-30. *A new project link!*

to the project home screen, as shown in Figure 6-30.

9. Now you need to add a few backlog items to work with, so I'm going to create a few quick user stories as an example, as shown in Figure 6-31. Items can easily be stack-ranked with your team by sliding them up and down the backlog and further broken down very quickly. Click the **Board** link when you are ready to see your backlog on the storyboard.

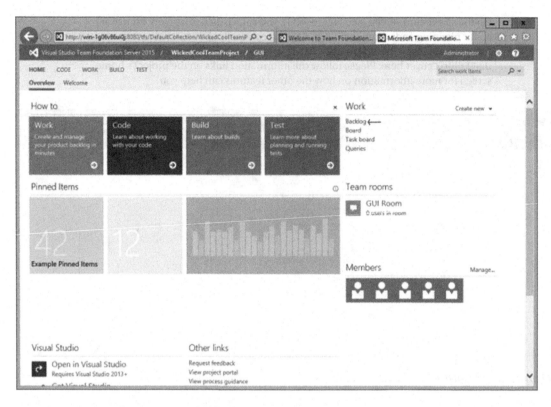

Figure 6-31. *Project home screen, select backlog*

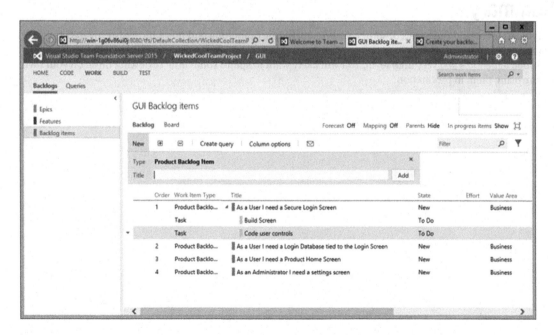

Figure 6-32. *Backlog screen allows you to quickly assemble an prioritize backlog*

10. On the storyboard screen (see Figure 6-33), you can visualize the work for use at sprint planning and scrum meetings. An item can easily slide to its accurate status for transparency in the team's work. There are many more agile tool functions that I didn't cover here. Please follow the information links on the project's home screen for more information on how the other features can help you.

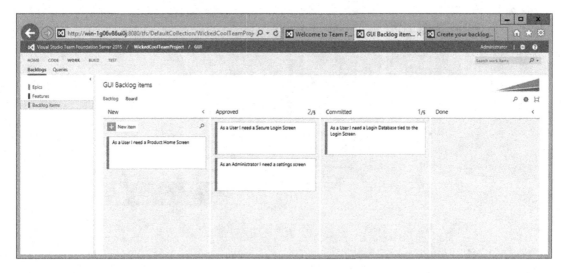

Figure 6-33. *Scrum board to status work quickly*

Summary

This chapter covered the basics of source control, including branching and merging. It also covered managing the associated work items (epics, stories, and bugs) and how to work with them using the included agile tools at a very high level. You will likely want to spend some time reviewing these on your own before using them in production.

CHAPTER 7

■ ■ ■

Maintaining Team Foundation Server

In the last chapter, we had some fun using TFS, so now seems a good time to talk about maintaining it. If you review the TFS architecture drawing in Figure 1-1, you will notice that TFS depends on a lot of components running properly to work. I'll cover some of the major points that you'll need to keep in mind while trying to keep your TFS environment healthy. You'll look at

- Operating system maintenance
- SQL maintenance
- TFS maintenance
- Backup

This might seem obvious, but every machine in your TFS system requires maintenance. Failure to do so might not only result in a failure and downtime, but a serious security breach that could put your company's IP (intellectual property) at risk or a system crash that could put you out of action for some time. Do I have your attention now? Great. Let's look at what you should be already doing.

Get Up to Date

There is a limit to what you can update (please refer to Chapter 1 for what is supported), and you want to do this prior to the TFS install, but generally, you want to be on the latest server OS release. This keeps you further away from obsolescence but also lets you take advantage of performance improvements that come out in each release.

Beyond this, you have to make sure that, at a minimum, the servers in your environment have been patched with all identified "critical" updates. This can be done with the Windows Update service that you use for your client OS updates (I recommend that you select just the critical ones to be automatically updated). Another alternative for larger environments is to set up the Windows Server Update Services (WSUS) on a server in your environment. This will give you complete control to approve which updates are applied to the servers. There is some overhead with this, so I would not recommend putting this on your sole TFS server. More information on WSUS is at https://technet.microsoft.com/en-us/windowsserver/bb332157.aspx. Also, if you can set up a schedule to never let more than 24 to 48 hours go by without an update check, you will be less vulnerable to 0-day attacks.

I will add a cautionary note here for SQL server. As mentioned in Chapter 1, there is a significant increase in the hardware requirements for SQL Server 2014 vs. SQL Server 2012 and back. I'm not saying don't upgrade to it—just make sure that you take into account the increase in requirements so that you are not caught off guard. More information is available in Chapter 1 and at https://msdn.microsoft.com/en-us/library/dd631889.aspx.

Disk Space

You need to keep a close eye on disk space for both the data tier and build servers. It can grow quickly, so as discussed in Chapter 1, you really can't have too much disk space. Unused and old workspaces also take up a lot of disk space. The best way to keep an eye on it is with Team Foundation Sidekicks, available at http://www.attrice.info/cm/tfs/. To clear up space, use **tf workspace /delete [/server:servername] workspacename[;workspaceowner]**. For the build servers, especially, you need to look at the build retention policies and the drop areas.

Security! Microsoft Baseline Security Analyzer (MBSA)

A secure server needs more than just updates. Ideally, you should examine a whole host of things, such as firewall settings and application configuration that may put your server at risk. This can be exhaustive. Another tool you can use to do an inspection of sorts on the server after the initial install and on a maintenance basis is the Microsoft Baseline Security Analyzer (MBSA). It is free and fairly easy to install and run. You can download and learn more about it at https://msdn.microsoft.com/en-us/library/dd631889.aspx. One very important feature of this tool is that, as the name implies, it creates a "baseline" report that you can use to compare with future runs. Put running this in your maintenance schedule.

Antivirus

Team Foundation Server has some specific antivirus settings to keep both it and your antivirus solution running at peak performance.

IIS Process Exclusion

You should exclude the Internet Information Services (IIS) worker process (w3wp.exe) if your AV solution doesn't support the process exclusion directly. The w3wp.exe process is usually at C:\Windows\System32\inetsrv\w3wp.exe. If it's not there, you can also locate this file by following these steps:

1. Make a TFS web request, such as by connecting to TFS through Team Explorer (you need to make sure that it's active).

2. On the Team Foundation Server application tier or proxy machine, select **Task Manager** and click the **Details** tab.

3. Locate w3wp.exe in the list of running processes.

4. Right-click **w3wp.exe** and then select **Open file location** to get to the location.

SQL and SharePoint

For SQL, you need to put in a few file and folder exclusions (DBs, log files, etc.). This is fairly involved and specific to a few versions. Full information on doing these exclusions are at https://support.microsoft.com/en-us/kb/309422. SharePoint has similar file exclusions. It's fairly extensive; it's located at https://support.microsoft.com/en-us/kb/952167.

SQL Maintenance

There are a number of touchpoints in maintaining a working high-performance SQL server that are way beyond the scope of this book, but I wanted to cover a few common ones here.

Backup

I didn't want you to think that I was skipping this; there is a whole section on it next. There is now a utility to set up the backup for TFS; the element is that whatever solution you use, it needs to utilize Transaction Marking in the process. Read up on it in the next section.

Run DBCC CHECKDB

You should regularly run DBCC CHECKDB to detect physical/logical corruption and get the best shot at cleanly repairing and preventing it. Full documentation on adding this to your maintenance script is in the MS SQL Server documentation and in a great blog post at `http://blogs.msdn.com/b/cindygross/archive/2010/06/13/dbcc-checkdb-database-integrity.aspx`.

Set PAGE_VERIFY=CHECKSUM

Make sure that PAGE_VERIFY=CHECKSUM is set to prevent corruption. Again, more on this one in the SQL documentation.

SQL ERRORLOG Monitoring

You'll want to monitor this log to look for errors before they become serious situations.

Backup

TFS backup is very near and dear subject to me. A bad TFS backup (unknown to me) was responsible for the failure of a valued customer to perform a restore. Do not begin any production installation or upgrade of any product mentioned here without a prior backup of all systems. Special attention should be paid to the backup of the Team Foundation Server system data tier. If done improperly, the backup will put your TFS installation into an unusable state after a restore operation; the worse part will be that you won't know this until you start using it again.

This is because during the DB backups, it is critical that all the timestamps of these backups are synchronized. Please review Microsoft's current recommendations on using marked transactions in your backup strategy (`https://msdn.microsoft.com/en-us/library/ms253151(v=vs.120).aspx`) if you are not going to use the Team Foundation Scheduled Backups Wizard (this tool builds that in). I'm often asked if a file system or "bare metal" backup is needed with TFS since most everything is in the databases. It is certainly possible to, just depend on reinstalling the software and restoring your databases to "recover" your TFS environment. However, you really should weigh the risk and the time involved. This is a bad place to try to save money.

Scheduled Backups Wizard

By far the easiest way to back up and restore your TFS database is with the Scheduled Backups Wizard. You access it in the Team Foundation Administration console.

1. Go to Start ➤ Microsoft Visual Studio Team Foundation Server 2015 ➤ Team Foundation Server Administration Console. From here go to the Scheduled Backups node, as shown in Figure 7-1. Click the **Create Scheduled Backups** link.

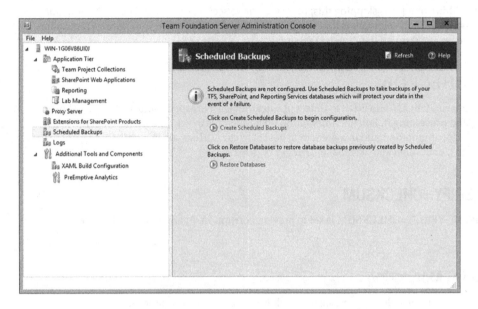

Figure 7-1. TFS Administration Console: Scheduled Backups

2. Next, you are brought to the first screen of the wizard, where you are prompted to select or type a network path to store your backups, as shown in Figure 7-2. You also have the option of changing the file extensions for the backup files. Here I'm just selecting a local share for demonstration purposes; in a production setting, you could select a NAS/SAN or other network location. Note that you must pick a network location; you will not be able to select a local folder directly. Click **Next** when ready.

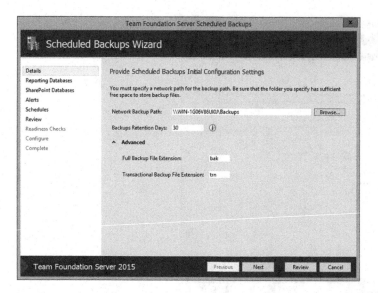

Figure 7-2. *Backup location*

3. Now you select to back up the Reporting Services DBs, as shown in Figure 7-3. For some reason, reporting databases are not selected by default; make sure that you select the option as indicated for a complete backup. You will also notice a new node opens below the current one to capture the Reporting Services Encryption Key. This is important to restoring your server.

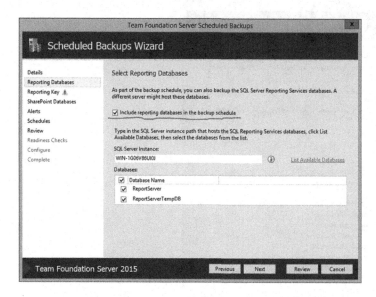

Figure 7-3. *Reporting databases*

4. Next, you need to back up the Reporting Key (you were prompted to save this in setting up Reporting Services). Don't have one? No worries, you can create one here too, as I'm doing in Figure 7-4. Either select or create one. Click **Next** when ready.

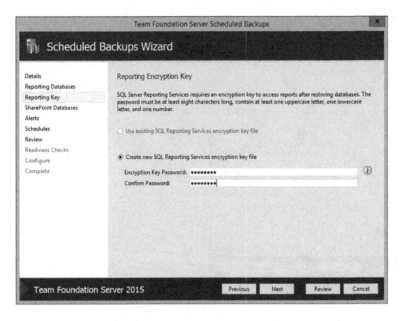

Figure 7-4. Reporting Encryption Key

5.   Now you need to select SharePoint databases, as indicated in Figure 7-5. (Again, for some reason this isn't selected by default.) Click **Next** when ready.

Figure 7-5. SharePoint databases

6.   On the next screen, you can configure e-mail alerts. These are grayed out here since I didn't set up e-mail on this installation, as shown in Figure 7-6.

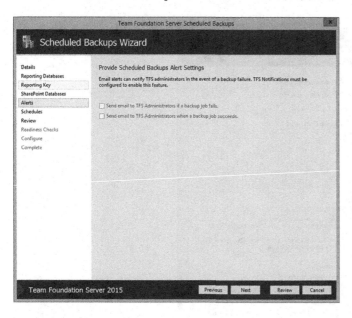

Figure 7-6. E-mail alerts

Next, you set the schedule. You can select a simple nightly, manual, or custom backup schedule, as I did as in Figure 7-7.

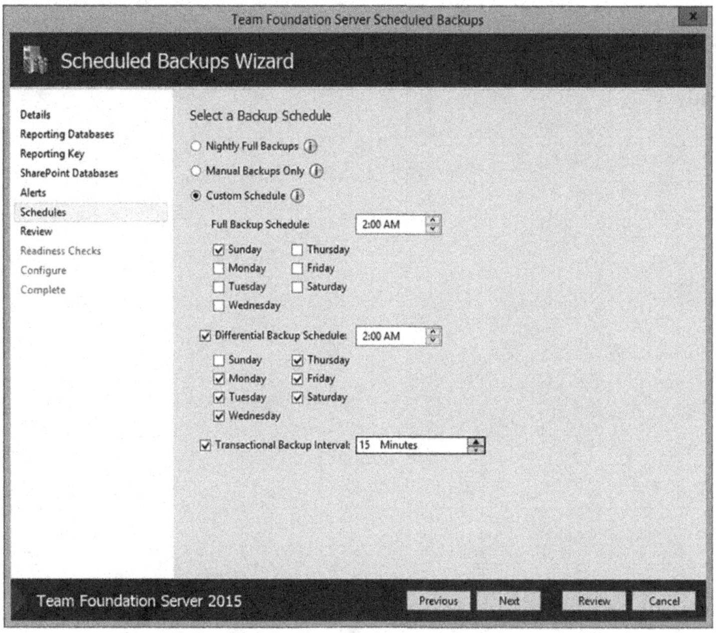

Figure 7-7. Schedules

7. Next is the Review screen, as shown in Figure 7-8. Review and click **Next** when ready.

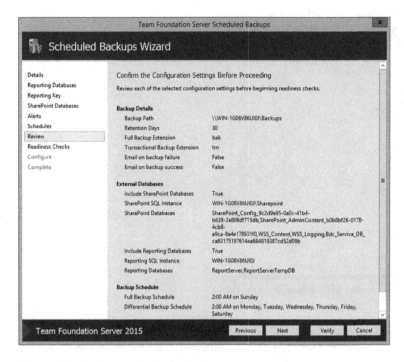

Figure 7-8. Review your backup schedule

8. The next screen (see Figure 7-9) features the Readiness checks. You can see that the checks are ready; if not, resolve the problems that you are prompted about. Click **Configure** when ready.

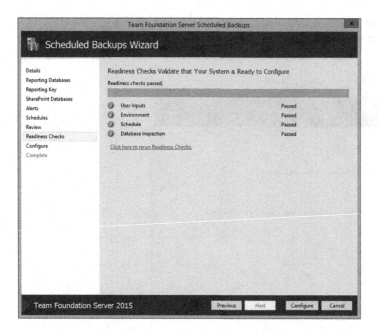

Figure 7-9. *Readiness Checks passed*

9. Next, you can see that the configuration ran fine, as shown in Figure 7-10. Click
    Next when ready.

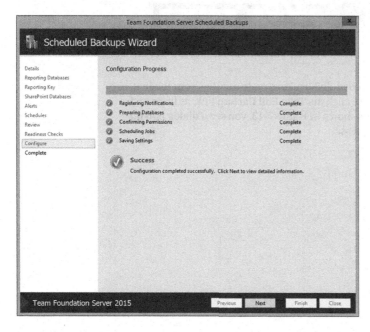

Figure 7-10. *Success!*

10. Lastly, you have the complete screen, as shown in Figure 7-11. Your backup is now scheduled as configured. Click **Close** when ready and return to the TFS Administration Console.

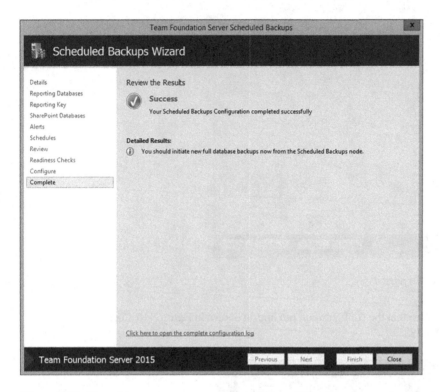

Figure 7-11. *Complete screen*

11. You can see now that our Scheduled Backups node now has your job in it, as shown in Figure 7-12. Please click the **Take Full Backup** link, as indicated, to complete the process. As shown in Figure 7-13, you see a dialog pop up, indicating the backup progress.

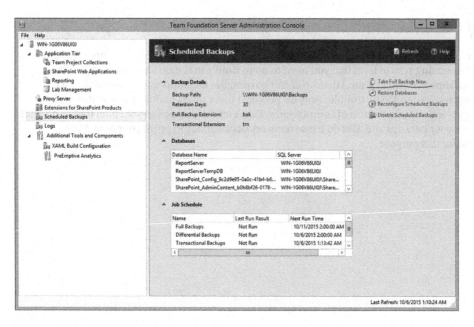

Figure 7-12. *Configured backup*

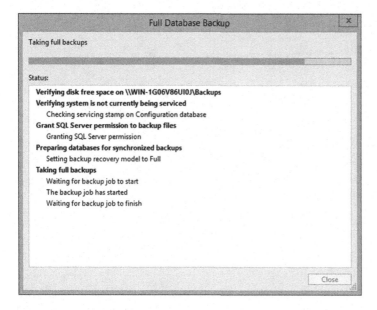

Figure 7-13. *Full backup progress*

Summary

This chapter covered the important points of maintaining your Team Foundation Server. There are some other items at the operating system level that you need to do to simply maintain a well-running system (normal system backups and patches, etc.) that we didn't go over, but are important as well. For some reason, backup and restore tend to be trouble spots for people. I think this is mainly because the reliability of systems these days lulls us into a sense of complacency. Don't let that happen to you: plan for the disaster you can't afford. Do your backups and also do a trial recovery occasionally to prove your plan. Virtual machines are great for this purpose.

CHAPTER 8

■ ■ ■

Build Management

This chapter looks at Team Foundation Build, which has gone through quite a facelift with a completely new build system. As we discussed in Chapter 3, Microsoft now gives us two completely different build systems. The new old XAML system and Team Foundation Build. Since we already checked out the XAML system while validating the system install, we'll stick with Team Foundation Build here and cover

- Setting up Team Foundation Build

- Multiplatform and customization

- Running unit tests and publishing results

- Continuous integration

Overview

So what are you looking at in Team Foundation Build 2015? A true multiplatform build system. You can now build Windows, iOS, Java (Maven, Ant, Grade), and Linux using any domain-specific language. Can you still use the legacy build system (now called XAML)? Sure, but if you are starting from scratch or making a small-scale upgrade, it would be worth your time to start making the transition to Team Foundation Build (TFBuild). You just need to have a build service and a build agent deployed locally (there is also the option of using Visual Studio Online's hosted build service, but that's beyond the scope of this book).

Setting up a Build Agent

You can run the following on your build server (which can also be your Team Foundation Server in a smaller environment) :

- Many agent pools (you can have many per Team Project Collection, set by platform, for instance, or one per collection)

- One or many build agents (depending on how much capacity you have, or use the VSO service) belonging to these pools

- Since you already set up build service on your local system (you did that by installing and running the Team Foundation Build service), you can skip that and go right to the good stuff.

Let's go through the steps of setting up Team Foundation Build since it takes a little work to get everything in place.

1. To begin, let's go back to the Team Web Access at `http://<tfs server name>:8080/tfs`. Click the gear icon on the top right of the page, as shown in Figure 8-1.

Figure 8-1. *Enter the Administration screen*

2. Next, let's look at the **Agent pools** tab, as shown in Figure 8-2. You can see the default Visual Studio Online (VsoBuildAgent) that was installed by default during the setup of the TFS server. That would be great, except that you want to build on premise and not use the cloud service. For this you need to install the agent. Click **Download agent** in the top left of the screen, as indicated. You will be prompted to save agent.zip. Save it to a local directory where you want to run it from. I created one called C:\LocalTFSBuild and saved it there.

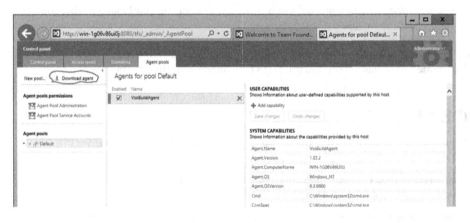

Figure 8-2. *Agent pools*

3. Once that's done, you need to extract the files (right-click and select **Extract all**). You see a file called `ConfigureAgent.ps1`. This is the configuration file you need to set up the agent. Right-click this file and select **Run ConfigureAgent.Ps1**. This pops open a PowerShell command window, as shown in Figure 8-3.

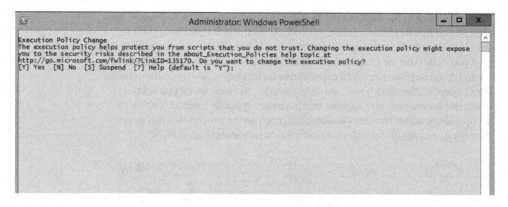

Figure 8-3. *PowerShell command window*

4. In the PowerShell window, answer Yes to the execution policy change (typically, you see this the first time you run PowerShell). Next, you are prompted to name the agent. You can write your own name or take the default, as I did. Now you need to enter the server URL. This is typically `http://<server name>:8080/tfs/`. If in doubt, refer to your Team Foundation Server Administration Console. Next, you need to enter the agent pool; you are using the default here, so just hit Enter. The work folder is next; hit Default to use the folder you saved the file in, or specify one. You are now prompted to run the agent as a service or interactively. Normally, service is the right choice but if you will be running a Coded UI test or need to debug a problem, interactive is the best choice. I chose interactive for this one, which left the command prompt open, as shown in Figure 8-4. This is normal and why service is better for a production environment. Do not close this window or else the agent will shut down; but you can minimize to get it out of the way.

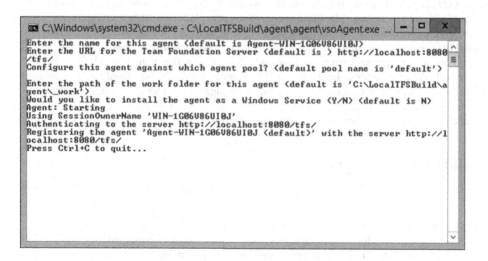

Figure 8-4. *Build Agent in a command window*

5. If you click back to the **Build** tab in the control panel, you see the new agent you created and that its status is green, as shown in Figure 8-5. From here you can enable or disable the agent as needed. You would have had more configuration to do if you didn't use the Default Collection, but this served as a good example to get started. You can also select **Add capabilities** on this tab to add more frameworks (like a specific .Net one). These are very powerful, because when you submit a build, the system only picks agents that have the capability needed. You've only set up a single agent here for Windows. You can use the procedures you've gone through to add agents for different platforms or frameworks as needed.

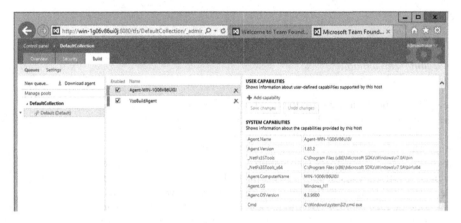

Figure 8-5. *The new tunning agent*

Scaling and Administering Team Foundation Build

You just configured a very simple Windows build agent on the default collection and default pool as an example. You co could also set up various Xplat build agents to support platforms other than Windows, as discussed earlier. More information on setting these up is available at https://msdn.microsoft.com/Library/vs/alm/Build/agents/xplat. In a production environment, you should consider a layout of various build agents hosted on their own virtual machines, which are on a series of dedicated build servers to host them. This would take a tremendous load off your TFS server (if you build there) and give you greater flexibility and redundancy. The System Center Virtual Machine Manager is great for this (configured from the TFS Administration Console) but a bit beyond what I can cover in the scope of this book. Let's now discuss how to go about the basic administration of Team Foundation Build.

Starting/Restarting Build Agents

Restarting a crashed or canceled configured build agent is easy. You don't need to reconfigure it, just launch it.

1. Start a PowerShell window (make sure you are an administrator), as shown in Figure 8-6. Switch to your local agent directory, which you configured the agent to; I went to C:\LocalTFSBuild\agent. Once there, just type **agent\VsoAgent.exe**. This restarts the agent as you already configured it. I configured an interactive one, so it starts in that mode, as shown. If you go to Control Panel ➤ Agent Pools, you should see your agent running (green status).

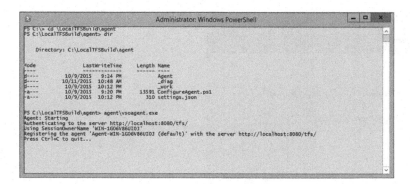

Figure 8-6. *PowerShell window to start agent*

Settings: Build Retention

The build retention policy is also set from the control panel. Launch it at http://<tfs server name>:8080/ tfs and click the gear icon on the top right if you don't already have it running. Select the **View collection administration page** link, and then the **Settings** link, as shown in Figure 8-7. The **Maximum Retention Policy: Days to keep** specifies that unless you specifically marked a build as Retain Indefinitely in the build definition file (discussed later), it's going to only keep for 30 days. This is fine for most teams, but if you have specific needs, you can adjust here.

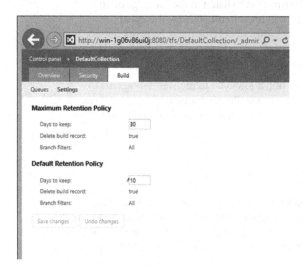

Figure 8-7. *Build Retention Policy*

Security: Letting Others Help Manage the Builds

One thing you will find out quickly once you move from building on the desktop to server-based builds with Team Foundation Build is that you will likely need to delegate some of this duty to other people, because setting up and managing agents for a team can be time intensive. This is done by going to the **Control panel ➤ Agent pools** tab. From there you can see two agent pool permissions: one for Agent Pool Administrators and another for Agent Service Pool service accounts. From there you can add to the groups, as pictured in Figure 8-8.

159

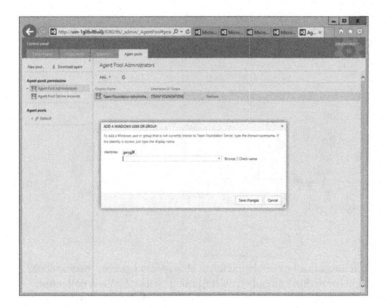

Figure 8-8. *Adding users to Agent Pool Administration Group*

- *Agent Pool Service Accounts*: Gives you permission to listen to the message queue for the specific pool to receive work. Except in rare circumstances, the agent registration process (like you went through) will suffice. Normally, Network Service is automatically added when you register the agent. You may need to consider adding an account here if you have specific enterprise security requirements.

- *Agent Pool Administrators*: Being in this group allows you to register new agents in the pool and add other users and service accounts. Put someone in this group if you need to delegate agent management activity. As with most security in TFS, you can add a Windows User Group or a TFS Group.

Using Team Foundation Build

Now you are going to look at using Team Foundation Build and walk through creating a simple Windows build. To begin, let's open the Team Web Access portal, typically at `http://<tfs server name>:8080/ tfs`. Click the Team Project link on the main page. I'm selecting the sample one I created earlier, the WickedCoolTeamProject. From here you click the Build link in the top tool bar, which should bring you to a similar screen to the one shown in Figure 8-9.

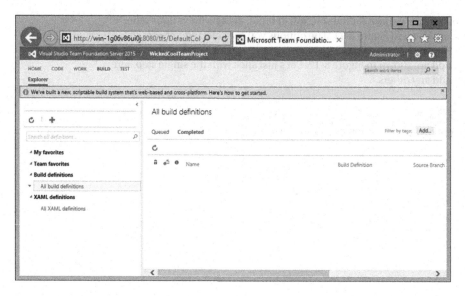

Figure 8-9. *Build main window*

Build Definitions: Creating and Queueing

The *build definition* defines how the build is laid out, what you want it to do, and with what code. It can also be set to trigger on certain events, such as a check-in or a clock. Do the following to create one.

1. Click the + sign in the top left. The first prompt is to select a template, as shown in Figure 8-10. More on this later, but you use templates to pre-fill common settings for both builds and deployments. You can see the defaults here (you can buy, download, or create more). I selected the Visual Studio for our walk through.

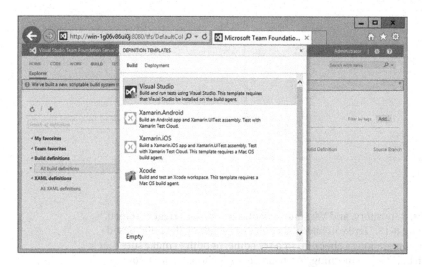

Figure 8-10. *Select a Build Definition template*

2. Next, you select a pattern for the solution to build, along with various other
    options, as shown in Figure 8-11. The options you see selected here are the
    default. Notice that you can add a build step here as well. Some of the steps that
    you can add are shown in Figure 8-12. Let's just stick with the single step here
    and not add any others.

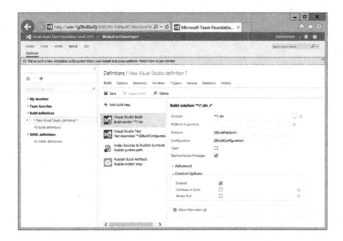

Figure 8-11. *Build step screen*

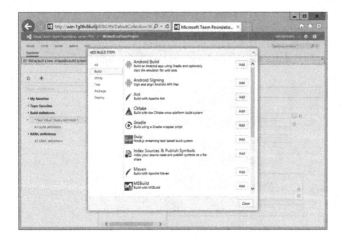

Figure 8-12. *Optional steps*

3. Skip the Options, Repository, and Variables screens. Select the **Triggers** screen,
    as shown in Figure 8-13. Here you have the choice of triggering the build based
    on a continuous integration (a check in) or a schedule, or both to make sure that
    you have a fresh build every morning, for instance. Let's choose Continuous
    Integration here. It also worth pointing out the Batch Changes option on this
    screen. It's on by default and important to leave it there since it prevents slightly
    overlapping builds.

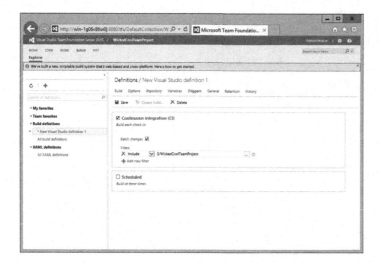

Figure 8-13. *Trigger selection*

4. Now is a good time to save. Hit the **Disk** button in the upper left of the screen and type a meaningful name, as shown in Figure 8-14.

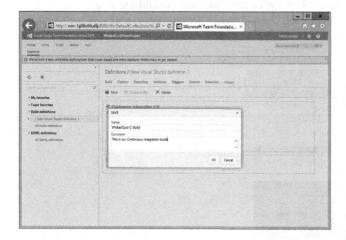

Figure 8-14. *Save the build definition*

5. Now you need to queue up the build definition that you just created so it will build when triggered. Select the **Queue build** link, as shown in Figure 8-15. On the dialog, you can see a lot of options, including selecting a particular shelve set, entering a build configuration, and in demands you could specify the existence of a file or files. This could be handy if you are depending on another build or system to deliver a component that you need to have finished before you build. For now, you are all set. Hit OK when you are ready to queue the build.

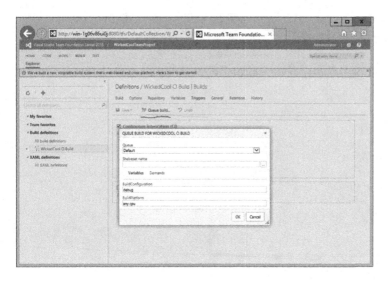

Figure 8-15. *Queue the build definition*

6. As soon as you hit OK, you are placed in the Build browser screen, where you see the build start up, the passed or failed steps on the left, and a console that shows the live results, as shown in Figure 8-16. In the future, you'll want to add a test or two to ensure code and build quality. All of these results are reportable and trackable.

Figure 8-16. *Build Explorer showing the build*

Summary

In this chapter you checked out the new build system and learned how to set up agents to perform builds. You also looked at setting build retention so that you don't fill up the build server and discovered what build definitions do.

CHAPTER 9

■ ■ ■

Testing with Team Foundation Server

Testing with Team Foundation Server has undergone many revisions and improvements over the years. Although most of the flashy testing features require a copy of Visual Studio (Enterprise or Test Professional), there are still several important testing functions that can be done with TFS on it its own. These testing functions are the focus of this chapter.

Testing your application is critical. Test early/test often is a mantra you hear from most agile teams, and for good reason—it's much easier to fix bugs while the code is still in active development. There are many testing tools available in both Visual Studio and TFS to support these efforts.

Do I Need Visual Studio for My Dedicated QA Team/Testers?

I get this question every time that a new release comes out. My answer was always *yes*, but with this latest release, I'm moving to a definite *maybe*. It really depends on how the work is organized and which tools the client needs to use. Let's begin with a quick overview of the available testing tools and what they can do for you. Table 9-1 breaks down the functionalities.

Table 9-1. *Testing Functionalities*

Testing scenario	Tool	Requires?
Test planning, management, and manual execution, including suites, cases, and steps	Team Web Access	TFS only
Recording steps and IntelliTrace data with the scenario above	Microsoft Test Manager	Visual Studio and TFS.
Integration/system-level tests run interactively	Coded UI test	Visual Studio and TFS (for results storage, tracking).
Continuous integration (CI) tests run at check-in or periodically	TFS build, coded UI, unit test, IntelliTest	Visual Studio (to create tests) TFS (to run / monitor).
Load and performance Testing	Load test	Visual Studio. TFS (for results storage, tracking.

As you can see, the two key testing features that you use with TFS are manual tests and continuous integration (CI) tests. It is worth noting that any test supported by Visual Studio can be run as a CI test, including coded UI tests (you need the agent to be in interactive mode to support this).

Next, you'll look at some of the testing that you can support with TFS alone.

Manual Test Planning, Creating, and Running

You are going to work in Team Web Access from here on. You can get to it from Visual Studio in the Team Web Access link in Team Explorer, or from your browser at `http://<tfs server>:8080/tfs/` (then select a Team Project shortcut).

1. Select the **Test** link. You should see the Test Hub window, as shown in Figure 9-1. Note the instructions on the screen, which is what you get in a Team Project without a test plan. You are going to take care of this next as you create a test plan. Click the **here** link to start (or you can click the + (plus sign) at the top of the left pane).

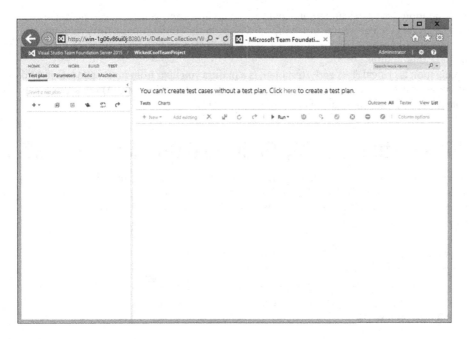

Figure 9-1. *Test hub*

2. Next, fill in the name of the test plan, as shown in Figure 9-2. The other information on this form is pre-filled. **Area path** is a hierarchal categorization method that TFS has had since the beginning. **Iteration** is designed to track releases and sprints. You used iterations in the chapter with storyboards (you can learn more on area paths and iterations at `https://msdn.microsoft.com/Library/vs/alm/Work/customize/modify-areas-iterations`). Currently, the area path is set to our Team Project and the iteration is set to the sprint you created previously. Hit **Create** when you've filled in the **Name** field. I called mine GUI Testing.

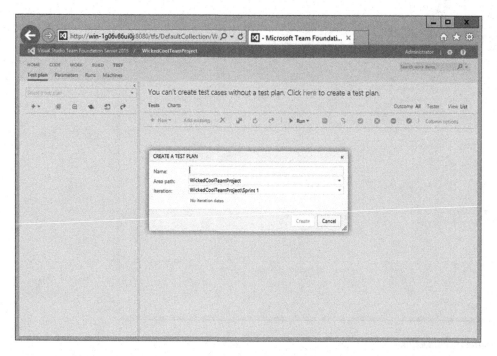

Figure 9-2. *Creating a test plan*

3. Now you'll need to create a test suite. You have some choices here, as indicated in Figure 9-3. You can create a static suite, a requirements-based suite, or a query-based suite. A *static suite* is pretty much how it sounds: just a suite based on whatever you enter. A *query-based suite* pops up a dialog to enter a work-item query. The *requirement-based suite* is what you'll use in this example. You use these to group test cases together so you can track the testing status of an item in the backlog. Each test case added to a requirement-based test suite is automatically linked to the backlog item. I really like these for that reason. Select **Requirement-based suite**.

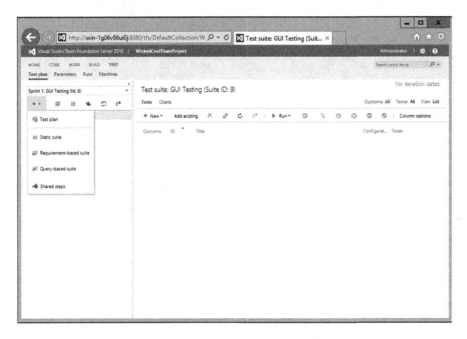

Figure 9-3. *Suite type selection*

4. Next, you are presented with a pre-populated work-item query screen of what's in the sprint. I'm going to select them all and build suites that link to them all at once, as pictured in Figure 9-4.

Figure 9-4. *Selecting all the sprint items*

5.   As you can see in Figure 9-5, the suites have been created. It's time to add a few steps. Select a suite and then click the **+New** drop-down list in the middle panel and select **New test case**. Note the option to create a **New test case from grid**. This is roughly like laying out a test case with an Excel sheet. Let's use the first one.

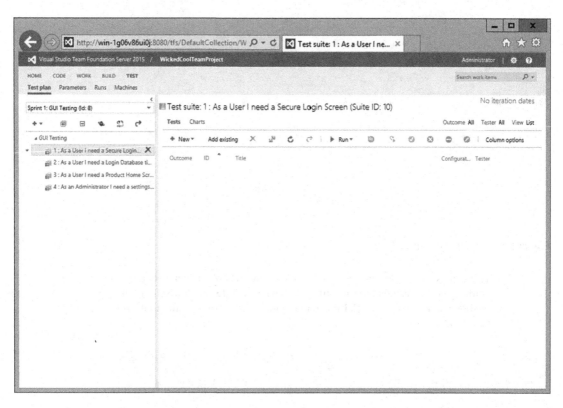

Figure 9-5. *Creating test cases for our suite*

6.   Next, I named the case and added some steps, as shown in Figure 9-6. Ordinarily, you'd have several test cases rolling up into several test suites, but what you have here now is fine to demonstrate the functionality. Click **Save** and close when ready.

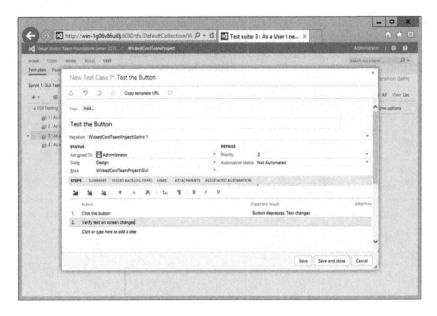

Figure 9-6. *Adding the case and steps*

7. This brings us back to the main test suite window, where you can see the status of the test case. As the cases are run, you can select if the step passed or failed, as shown in Figure 9-7. Click **Run** so that you can see the steps and mark some results on a few.

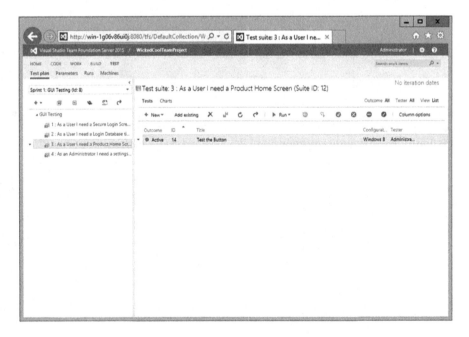

Figure 9-7. *Main test case view*

8. Next, you are going to perform each step and mark a few as passed or failed. Note that as you clicked Run on the test case page, the web-based Test Runner popped up (see Figure 9-8) and took its position on the left side of the screen, where it will be out of the way but keep the test steps handy. It runs on all the major browsers—Internet Explorer, Chrome, Firefox, and Safari. You can move it around as needed as well. There are controls on the side of the test steps to mark as pass, fail, or record a comment. The few at the top record the results, create a bug, and save. Let's mark a few steps here as pass or fail, record the results, and click **Save and close**. I'm going to do this a few times to get a mix of results to look at.

Figure 9-8. *Test Runner*

9. When you go back to the test hub, you see that our test case has a "passed" indicator near it. To see the individual runs, click the **Run** link at the top of the left panel. This shows you the individual test runs. You can see in Figure 9-9 that I recorded a few failures as well.

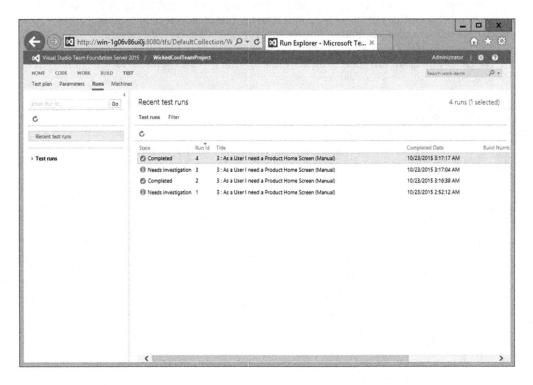

Figure 9-9. *Test runs*

10. Next, let's look at a chart of the test results. First, you need to build it. Go to **Test plan ➤ Graph**. This section is empty until you create a chart, so let's do that. Click the **+New** drop-down list and select the Test Results chart. You should see a screen like the one shown in Figure 9-10. I'm choosing to create a pie chart and to sort by Outcome, but there are several other choices here. Click **OK** when ready.

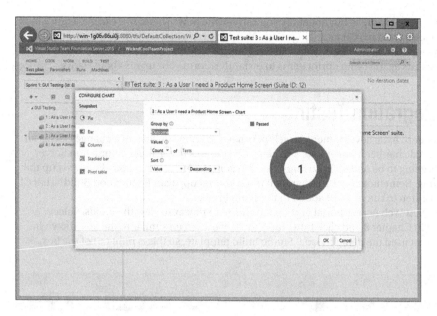

Figure 9-10. *Building a test runs chart*

11. In the chart view, you can see the test results, as shown in Figure 9-11.

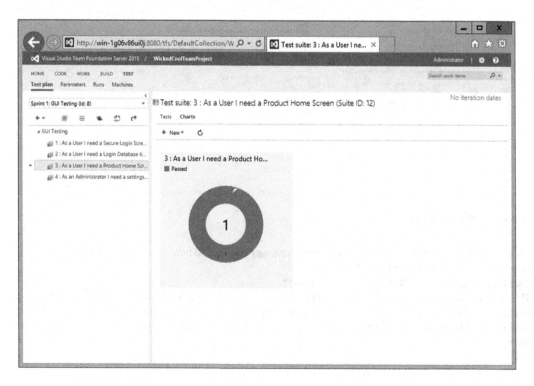

Figure 9-11. *Test results chart*

Now this was a very simple example, but hopefully you can see the power here. You can get a quick look across the entire sprint backlog and look at its testing status. You can even pin this chart to the home page by clicking the **...** icon in the top right of the chart. That's all I'm going to cover here. You now have the tools to create a complete suite of tests against your sprint items to instantly inform your teams about status.

Continuous Integration Testing

To support the pace of modern agile development, developers need to know the instant a change causes an error, or when some new code has been integrated. You can deliver this using Team Foundation Server and Visual Studio. This is going to be one of those times that I'm going to tell you that you already set up the framework to run CI testing. Remember back in Chapter 8 when you set up Team Foundation Build? That CI build that you set up had a step to run *any* test added to the Team Project.

Let's go back to the Team Web Access portal and click **Build ➤ Explorer** to view the builds. Select the build that you created in Chapter 8 and click **Edit**. You should see a screen similar to the one shown in Figure 9-12. If you recall, you used the default Visual Studio build template, so this is right out of the box.

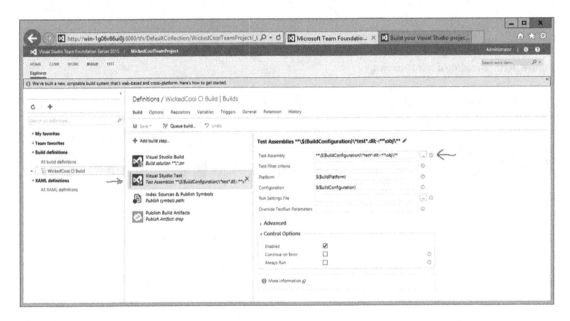

Figure 9-12. *CI build test step*

Looking at the current build's test step configuration, as I've selected here, you can see the Test Assembly parameter that lets the build do its stuff:

*\\\$(BuildConfiguration)*test*.dll;-:**\obj*

This combination of wild cards has the effect of running any version of Visual Studio you drop in the Team Project. It will run any DLL with "test" in its name, except in object directories. Pretty cool, right? Well, most of the time it is, but just keep in mind what this line is looking for—and not looking for—to run the tests that you want.

For example, I like to run coded UI tests in my build process. So as long as I'm running my agents in interactive mode, that's great. However, if I didn't have my agents set up that way, or if I had coded UI, unit, or other test types that were not ready for production, or are unsuitable to run on a build agent, my build would fail as soon as I checked them in. The solution to this is to exclude the non-production test paths from the test assembly path, like the obj one is. Not a big deal if you are ready for it.

Summary

You covered a lot of ground quickly in this unit. You looked at using the Test Runner with Team Web Access. You also walked through planning your manual tests suites and tying them to the requirements that should be driving them.

■ ■ ■

CHAPTER 10

Reporting and Other Features Worth Exploring

The reporting functionality (in addition to the dashboards that you've looked at) in Team Foundation Server is provided through SQL Reporting Services. It's very powerful and expandable. In this chapter, you'll look at the reporting functionality and what the system offers at a high level. I'll also discuss some areas that you may want to explore for further research. This chapter covers

- Reporting functionality

- Types of reports available

- Report security and administration

- Other TFS features that you should explore

- Reporting

There are a number of different reporting platforms available with TFS. What you choose depends on what you are looking for. For instance, SharePoint dashboards are great for visualizing data sets that you want to monitor constantly, but take some work to set up and modify. On the other end of the scale are work-item queries that are quick and simple, but offer little in terms of graphics for visualization. Let's have a look at these to see what makes sense for you to use.

SQL Reporting Services Reports

The out-of-the-box SQL Reporting Services reports are quite good and cover most areas you'd want to keep an eye on, such as work progress and bugs. A handy feature (which you'd be smart to include in your custom reports) is a link to related reports that the viewer might want to check out. These include parameters to make the reports more flexible, such as filtering by area paths and iterations.

Your actual collection of reports will vary based on the process template you chose for the project. Figure 10-1 shows a sample Backlog Overview Report, for example. There isn't much activity in this example system, but you can imagine how useful a report like this could be in monitoring organization-wide development deliverables and test results. Other reports include the build status and test case readiness. Of the visual reports, these are the easiest to customize as well with a little knowledge of SQL Reporting Services. You can browse all of the reports by going to the Reports service in your deployment, normally at `http://<report server:80/Reports`, but you can always check the Team Foundation Server ➤ Application Tier ➤ Reporting.

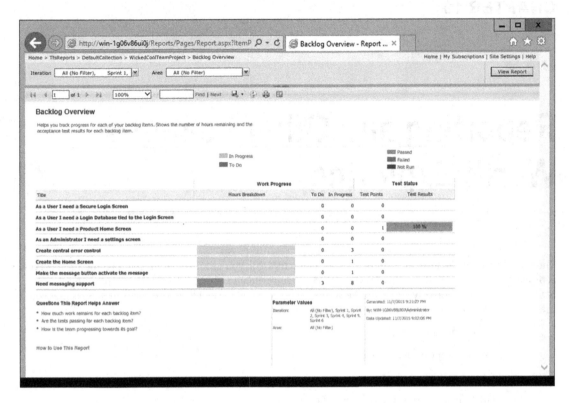

Figure 10-1. *Backlog Overview report*

One thing worth mentioning in a recovery or crash scenario is that the SQL Analysis Services may require you to rebuild the warehouse. There is a fairly simple way to do this. Just go to Team Foundation Server Administration Console ➤ Application Tier ➤ Reporting. Click the **Rebuild** link, as indicated in Figure 10-2. This rebuilds the warehouse and gets your reports back in working order.

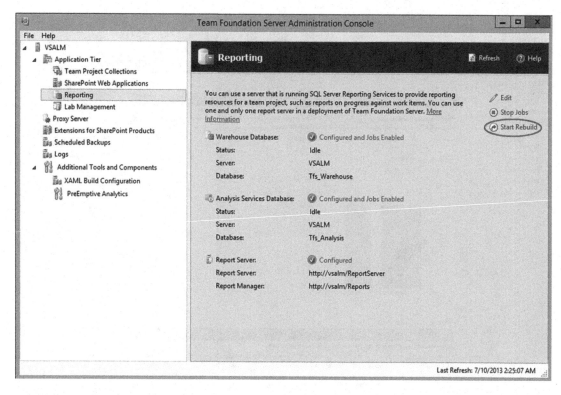

Figure 10-2. *Rebuilding the warehouse*

SharePoint Dashboards

What you get from SharePoint dashboards varies based on what you chose as a process during the creation of the Team Project. Scrum, for instance, only offers a Release dashboard, whereas Agile offers the My Dashboard and the Project, Progress, Quality, Test, Bugs, and Build dashboards. However, what you get also varies by which version of SharePoint is integrated; there is a notable difference between SharePoint Standard Edition and SharePoint Server Enterprise. Your best bet is to review the article at https://msdn.microsoft.com/library/dd380719.aspx if a specific dashboard is important to you. These dashboards are built from a combination of Excel reports and Team Project data. Since Scrum was chosen for our process, you only get the Release dashboard; however, this board has just about everything that you need to keep an eye on, including the burndown, backlog, and stats on work items, recent builds, and check-ins. You can always add or move around the web parts on the page if the Release dashboard doesn't quite suit you. A sample Release dashboard is shown in Figure 10-3.

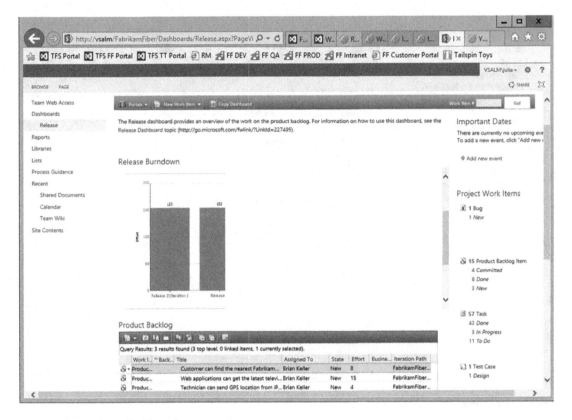

Figure 10-3. Release dashboard

Excel Reports

The Excel reports are used throughout the Dashboards, so likely you are already using them and just don't know it. TFS also provides an Excel template that you can use to query anything in the data warehouse. If you have the Enterprise edition of SharePoint, your portal comes with a selection of Excel reports to track bugs, tests, and other deliverables. However, you can roll your own reports with the Excel template provided. Figure 10-4 shows a simple work item–based report.

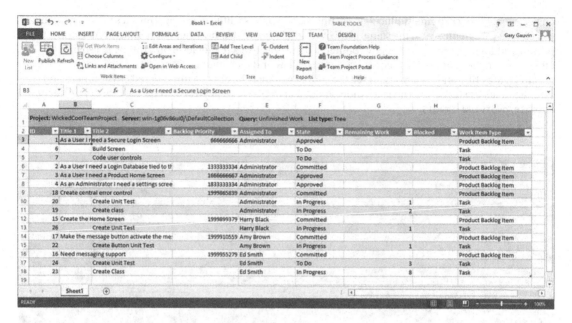

Figure 10-4. Excel-based work item report

Other TFS Features You Should Explore

Unfortunately, when you are writing an essentials book on a tight deadline, you just don't have the bandwidth to include every feature that TFS has to offer, even at a high level. I want to briefly introduce you to a few areas that I think you should research on your own to see if these features might add value to your deployment. There are certainly more features, but I find the following to be the most interesting, and I think you might too.

Lab Management

Lab Management is TFS's virtual machine build management system. It can be used in conjunction with build management and testing, providing the provisioning or build and test configurations as needed. It is by no means an essential element; I deploy it for clients only about half the time. When I don't deploy it, it's because the client really didn't need what it had to offer (too small an operation) or they already had a competitive solution that was working fine for them. You can use Lab Management to manage both standard environments (physical and single machine virtual machines of any type) and SCVMM (System Center Virtual Machine Manager) environments that can be multitier Hyper-V machines (just Hyper-V, actually). It can be configured in the Team Foundation Administration Console. You can read up on it a little more at https://msdn.microsoft.com/en-us/library/dd936084.aspx.

Release Management

Release Management is an interesting new product to the TFS family. It lets you automate your deployment process across all of your environments directly from your continuous integration builds. It lets you stage your environments and create an approval-based workflow so that transitions from, let's say, development to testing to production are planned, and not happening by accident or by the sheer momentum that happens on occasion. It's not extremely difficult to set up; it just requires a little planning. Once it's up and running, you can keep a careful eye on the status of all of your releases and know where something went astray. It provides additional traceability on environments that may need a higher level of scrutiny. It also makes otherwise complex deployment sequences easy to follow and repeatable.

In Figures 10-5 and 10-6, you can see the simple workflow layout of a three-tiered environment and a library of release tasks. You can learn more about it at https://msdn.microsoft.com/Library/vs/alm/Release/overview-rm2015.

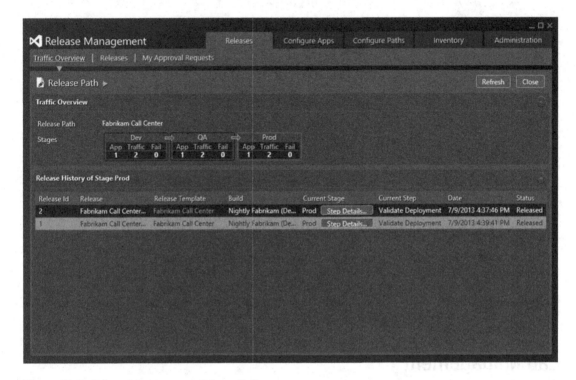

Figure 10-5. *Release Management: Release Path*

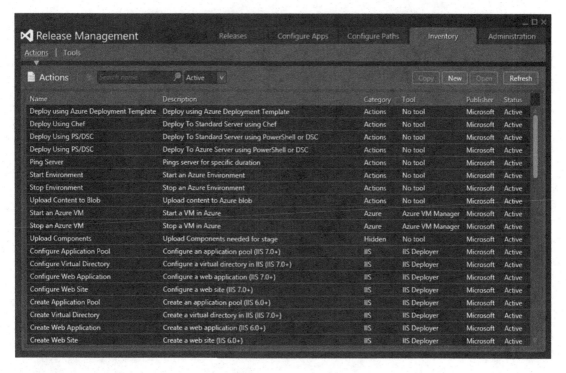

Figure 10-6. *Release Management: actions you can reuse consistently*

ALM Virtual Machines

So, this is not technically a feature but I feel compelled to mention it. Visual Studio ALM virtual machines—initially built by Brian Keller at Microsoft—are an extremely valuable resource for learning more about TFS and Visual Studio. You can use them to see what a fully configured system with sample data looks like. There is also a collection of hands-on labs that you can use to become more familiar with the features in a safe environment. I've used these in the past and they have been of real value to me. I even used them for a few screenshots in this book. You can learn more at `http://vsalmvm.azurewebsites.net/alm-vm-2015-available-now/`.

One thing you won't learn at that web site is that you can actually use the Oracle VM VirtualBox freeware application to host it just about anywhere—in addition to a Hyper-V environment. Simply configure the VM as stated for Hyper-V, but in VirtualBox. In older releases, you had to move the VHD file to an IDE virtual controller, but as of version 5.0.8 r103449, the default SATA controller seems to work just fine. You can see mine running in Figure 10-7.

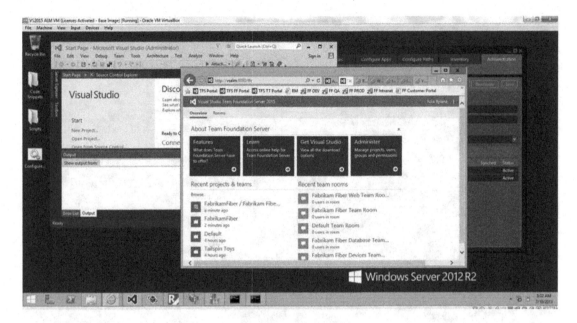

Figure 10-7. *The Visual Studio ALM VM running on a VirtualBox VM*

Summary

This chapter covered reporting and a few other areas that I think you should explore. I hope that you found this book useful in your exploration of Team Foundation Server 2015. It is far from an exhaustive work, but it should at least get you started and let you know where you should dig deeper. Team Foundation Server is a force multiplier in the development world and a rare one that can help a small five-person development team sort out the chaos of quick-moving projects. It can also help a large enterprise maintain consistent practices.

Index

■ A

ALM virtual machines, 183
Antivirus
    IIS process exclusion, 144
    SQL and SharePoint, 144

■ B

Build management
    administration screen, 156
    agent pools, 156
    build, definition
        Build Explorer, 164
        queue, 164
        save, 163
        step screen, 162
        template, 161
        trigger selection, 163
    command window
        build agent, 157
        PowerShell, 157
    PowerShell command window, 156
    Team Foundation
        build retention policy, 159
        security, 159–160
        starting/restarting build agents, 158
        tunning agent, 158
Build Service configuration
    Administration Console and Build
        Configuration, 62
    agents, 55
    Configuration Center, 52
    Configuration complete, 59
    CPU and RAM, 50
    disk subsystem, 50
    new build server installation, 51
    readiness checks, 58
    Review settings, 57
    service account selection, 56
    summary screen, 61

Team Foundation Build Service dialog, 53
Team Project Collection, 54

■ C

Collection management
    architecture, 67–68
    containers, 67
    databases, 68
    naming conventions, 69
    resources, 68
    team projects, 68
Continuous Integration (CI) Testing, 174–175

■ D

Detaching progress, 81–82

■ E, F, G

Excel reports, 180–181

■ H

HTTPS. *See* Hypertext Transfer Protocol
        Secure (HTTPS)
Hypertext Transfer Protocol
        Secure (HTTPS), 62

■ I, J, K

Installation, TFS
    advanced upgrade, 19–20
    Application Tier, 14
    basic services, 14
    category, 13
    location, selection, 21
    media selection, 20
    negotiate authentication, 14
    new installation, 13
    progress screen, 21–22

Installation, TFS (*cont.*)
  standard single server
    items configuration, 14–15
    wizard selection, 22–23
  upgrades, 14
  workflow, 14
Installation validation
  Logs directory, 49–50
  Server URLs
    services and web, 45
    Web Access Admin screen, 48
    Web Access main page, 47
    Web Access URL, 46
  services, 48–49

■ L

Lab management, 62, 74, 181

■ M, N, O, P, Q

Microsoft baseline security analyzer (MBSA), 144
Microsoft Developer Network (MSDN), 1

■ R

Release management server, 181, 183
Reporting functionality, TFS
  Excel reports, 180–181
  SharePoint dashboards, 179–180
  SQL reporting services reports, 177, 179

■ S

Secure Sockets Layer (SSL), 62
Security, TFS
  Active Directory groups, 62–63
  default groups, 64
  HTTPS, 62
  on-hold project, 64
  SSL, 62
  users and groups, 61–63
  VPN, 62
  Web access, 64
SharePoint dashboards, 179–180
SharePoint Requirements
  SharePoint 2010, 8, 15
  SharePoint 2013, 1, 8, 93
Source code management
  local workspaces, 120
  server workspaces, 119
  Source Control Explorer
    branching, 129–130
    check in and out, 128
    merging, 130, 132

team project
  adding solution to source control, 125
  folder name, location confirmation, 126
  Source check box, 124
  Source Control Explorer, 127
workspace set up
  configuration, 121–122
  local path defined, 123
  mapped notification, 123
SQL maintenance
  backup, 145
  DBCC CHECKDB, 145
  ERRORLOG monitor, 145
  PAGE_VERIFY=CHECKSUM, 145
SQL reporting services reports, 177, 179
SQL Server requirements
  high availability (HA), 10
  Server Express, 9
  SQL Server 2012, 8
  SQL Server 2014, 8–9
SSL. *See* Secure Sockets Layer (SSL)

■ T

Team Foundation Server 2013 (TFS 2013)
  architecture
    high availability (HA), 2
    scaled-out servers, 2
  installation
    64-bit server operating system (OS), 3
    accounts and permissions, 4–6
    checklist, 3–4
    Server Core installation, 3
    Server operating systems, 6–7
  language requirements, 12
  MSDN, 1
  ports
    alternation, 11
    default, 11
  scaling and performance, 7
  SharePoint requirements, 8
  single-server installation, 8
  SQL Server requirements, 8, 10
  TFS DB, 10
  Visual Studio 2013, 1
Team Foundation Server maintenance
  antivirus, 144
  backup
    configured backup, 152–153
    e-mail alerts, 149
    location, 147
    readiness checks, 151
    reporting encryption key, 148
    reporting services DBs, 147
    reviewing schedule, 150

scheduled backups, 146, 149
    SharePoint databases, 148
disk space, 144
MBSA, 144
SQL maintenance, 145
WSUS, 143
Team Foundation Server, testing
    functionalities, 165
    Team Web Access
        sprint items selection, 168
        suite type selection, 167–168
        test cases creation, 169
        test case view, 170
        test hub, 166
        test plan creation, 166–167
        test results chart, 173
        test runner, 171
        test runs chart, 172–173
Team Foundation Version
    Control (TFVC), 110
Team project collections
    administrators group, 70
    attach collection feature, 83
    collection database, 87
    complete detachment, 82–83
    configuration review, 75
    configuration success, 76
    confirmation, 89
    database creation, 72
    Database Wizard, 85
    data tier, 69
    default collection, 69
    default SQL Server, 71
    deployment, 69
    detach collection, 78
    environments, 71
    familiar screen, 83–84
    Farm Administrators group, 77, 86
    important projects, 71
    lab management, 74
    List Available Databases, 86
    maintenance operations, 70
    moved collection, 92
    naming conventions, 71
    readiness checks, 76, 80–81, 90
    report collections, 92–93
    reports location, 73
    server documentation, 84
    Server Management Studio, 85
    servicing message, 78
    SharePoint collections, 93, 95
    SharePoint products, 77
    SharePoint Site, 72
    site collection, 94, 96

    splitting, 96
    SQL backup utility, 84
    stricter environment, 73
    target server, 86
    verification tests, 79
    warning log, 90–91
    web application, 72
Team projects management
    administrators group account
        administer panel, 105
        group membership, 107
        web access control panel, 106
        Windows user\group dialog, 108
    Git, 110
    naming conventions, 98
    project collection to relationship, 97
    reports
        home page, 99
        role assignment entry screen, 101
        security, 100
    security, 110
    SharePoint permissions, 108–109
    SQL server database
        database engine connection, 102
        database role properties, 103
        user addition, 104
        user selection, 104
    team project boundaries, 98
    TFS process support, 110
    TFVC, 110
    Visual Studio 2015
        process template selection, 114
        project, 112
        project created confirmation, 117, 118
        project name and description, 113
        SharePoint site, 115
        source control selection, 116
        team explorer, 111
        TFS Server dialog, 112
TFS databases
    Active Directory, 11
    functional levels, 11
    Windows NT Server 4.0, 10
    TFVC. *See* Team Foundation Version
        Control (TFVC)

■ U

Upgrades, TFS
    back up, 16
    in-place upgrade, 18–19
    installer, selection, 17
    older releases, 16
    options, selection, 15

Upgrades, TFS (*cont.*)
    path, 15–16
    performance, advanced upgrade, 19–20
    prerequisites, 15
    SharePoint/SQL Reporting Services, 16
    SQL server, 16
    steps
        backup, 17
        latest service packs, 17
        requirement, analysis, 17
        uninstall, TFS 2010, 17
    option selection, 17–18

■ V

Virtual private network (VPN), 63
Visual Studio 2013. *See* Team Foundation
        Server 2013 (TFS 2013)
VPN. *See* Virtual private network (VPN)

■ W, X, Y, Z

Windows Server Update Services (WSUS), 143
Work management
    project
        administration screen, 134
        link, 140
        screen, 134
        selection, 133
    Team Foundation Server
        administration, selection, 133
        backlog screen, 141
        backlog selection, 141
        iterations/sprints and options, 140
        pick settings, 138
        scrum board, 142
        team dialog creation, 135
        user addition, 136–137
WSUS. *See* Windows Server Update Services (WSUS)

Get the eBook for only $5!

Why limit yourself?

Now you can take the weightless companion with you wherever you go and access your content on your PC, phone, tablet, or reader.

Since you've purchased this print book, we're happy to offer you the eBook in all 3 formats for just $5.

Convenient and fully searchable, the PDF version enables you to easily find and copy code—or perform examples by quickly toggling between instructions and applications. The MOBI format is ideal for your Kindle, while the ePUB can be utilized on a variety of mobile devices.

To learn more, go to www.apress.com/companion or contact support@apress.com.

Printed in the United States
By Bookmasters